John Smith: An Appreciation

John Smith:
An Appreciation

Edited by Christopher Bryant

Hodder & Stoughton
LONDON SYDNEY AUCKLAND

First published in Great Britain in 1994 by Hodder and Stoughton
A Division of Hodder Headline PLC

British Library Cataloguing in Publication Data

A Record for this book is available from the British Library

ISBN 0 340 62801 4

Typeset by Hewer Text Composition Services, Edinburgh
Printed and bound in Great Britain by
Cox & Wyman, Reading, Berks.

Hodder and Stoughton Ltd,
A division of Hodder Headline PLC
338 Euston Road
London NW1 3BH

After this it was noised abroad that Mr Valiant-for-Truth was taken with a summons, and had this for a token that the summons was true, *That his pitcher was broken at the fountain*. When he understood it, he called for his friends, and told them of it. Then said he, 'I am going to my fathers, and though with great difficulty I am got hither, yet now I do not repent me of all the trouble I have been at to arrive where I am. My sword, I give to him that shall succeed me in my pilgrimage, and my courage and skill, to him that can get it. My marks and scars I carry with me, to be a witness for me that I have fought his battles who will now be my rewarder.'

When the day that he must go hence was come, many accompanied him to the River side, into which, as he went, he said, 'Death, where is thy sting?' and as he went down deeper, he said, 'Grave where is thy victory?'

So he passed over, and all the trumpets sounded for him on the other side.

John Bunyan (1628–88)

The words of the anthem sung at John Smith's memorial service at Westminster Abbey on 14th July 1994.

Contents

Foreword

The second commandment calls upon us to love our neighbours as ourselves. It does not expect a frail humanity to be capable of loving our neighbours more than ourselves: that would be a task of saintly dimension. But I do not believe we can truly follow that great commandment unless we have a concept of care and concern for our fellow citizens which is reflected in the organisation of our society. In this vital way we can ally our Christian faith to our democratic socialist conviction. In the pursuit of both we can aspire to lead our country to find the real wealth which only a good society can provide.

With these words John Smith ended his Tawney lecture in March 1993. They are words that reflect both a quiet self-confidence and a clear sense of determination. Both of these were vital aspects of his work as a junior Minister, as Shadow Chancellor and especially as Leader of the Labour Party.

They also betray, however, a genuine humility about the task of politics, and about our human condition, a humility which would have fought shy of any sense of pomp or an overblown sense of his own importance, in life and in death.

This book is written, therefore, not as an attempt to capture John Smith's full contribution to our national life, nor indeed as a simple biographical evaluation.

Instead it is a genuine attempt to do three things: to remember what John Smith stood for, to hint at some of the measure of the man, and to carry the vision forward. Some of those who write here were close personal friends and colleagues. Others were companions in the Shadow Cabinet. Others again had less contact with him, but shared his deep personal conviction in that particular brand of ethical socialism that was Christian. While the early chapters are written very personally about that friendship later chapters are focused more clearly on the task ahead of the Labour Party, the Christian Socialist Movement, and our nation.

What this book is also is a follow-up to the book of essays *Reclaiming the Ground* in which John Smith's Tawney lecture was published, and to which several of those who write here also contributed. Most of them, though not all, are members of the Christian Socialist Movement, to which John Smith belonged. What all of us share is our sense of the dynamic imperative for an ethical socialism. So this book is written in the belief that the ideals that John Smith stood for, and in particular his understanding of the moral basis of Labour's political task, are vital for the genuine renewal of our national life.

Again he said, 'I believe we must argue for our cause on the basis of its moral foundation. It is a sense of revulsion at injustice and poverty and denied opportunity, whether at home or abroad, which impels people to work for a better world, to become, as in our case, democratic socialists.' Yet it would be wrong for any appreciation of John Smith to be exclusively Christian, and this book is not. Referring to R.H. Tawney he himself said, 'His Christian faith, which I am glad to share, was the foundation of his approach. But he did not claim – nor should any Christian – that only Christianity could provide the moral framework for an ethical approach to politics.' This book, then, seeks to reflect some of the breadth of John Smith's fuller vision.

Finally I should say, as one who respected John Smith more than knew him, that this book was put together out of simple tribute, and out of a belief that his work must go on.

At the end of Grahame Greene's *Mosignor Quixote* the atheist Communist Mayor, who has just buried his friend the priest, drives away from the church,

> The Mayor didn't speak again before they reached Orense; an idea quite strange to him had lodged in his brain. Why is it that the hate of a man – even of a man like Franco – dies with his death, and yet love, the love which he had begun to feel for Father Quixote, seemed now to live and grow in spite of the final separation and the final silence – for how long, he wondered with a kind of fear, was it possible for that love of his to continue? And to what end?'

Britain was clearly surprised by the depth of its feelings when John Smith died, surprised perhaps in part because it had not realised it could so value a politician. Yet what he stood for, his passionate defence of the most vulnerable, his desire to see justice, his insistence on the role of the State in strengthening the freedom of the individual by strengthening communities, his commitment to a democratic, ethical, international socialism, all these must live on in the policies and in the life of the Labour Party and the nation.

In his foreword to *Reclaiming the Ground* John Smith's successor, Tony Blair, wrote, 'To radicals it [Christianity] has always had an especial validity. Radicals want change, and change, both personal and social, lies at the heart of the Christian religion.' Undoubtedly the greatest possible tribute to John Smith will be radical social, political, economic change in Britain. Again in the words of Tony Blair, 'when we look at our world today and how much needs to be done, we should not hesitate to make such judgements. And then follow them with determined action. That would be Christian Socialism.'

Chris Brayant

1

Leading and Opposing

Hilary Armstrong was elected MP for Durham North West in 1987, and is a member of Labour's National Executive Committee. Having been an opposition spokesperson on Education from 1988 to 1992, she was John Smith's PPS until his death. She is a Vice-President of the National Children's Homes and of the Christian Socialist Movement.

There are two obvious significant components to being Leader of the Opposition. First it is important to lead, and second it is important to oppose. John Smith was very good at both, although frequently got impatient with 'opposing'.

Leading an organisation calls for a wide range of skills, but they must all be bundled together around a character which at his or her very core, knows what they are doing, and importantly why they are doing it. Good leadership involves thousands and thousands of small decisions which move institutions in a coherent direction – so it means that lots of day-to-day little matters must be added up into an overall motion in the same direction.

1

Working closely with John as his Parliamentary Private Secretary for the time of John's leadership meant that I saw him make those thousands of small decisions about where to lead our Party, and our society. I also saw him be clear about what were the really important decisions, where he really had to dig his heels in, and what were the issues that he could simply support other people on. What line should he take with De Klerk from South Africa over a year before the date for multi-racial elections had been set? How should he deal with a member of the Parliamentary Labour Party who feels they should have been promoted but were not? Should he force the Prime Minister to the despatch box in a debate? Can he miss Prime Minister's Question Time for a meeting of the Socialist International? In the charade of Prime Minister's Question Time, should he follow the issue of the day, or try to catch the Prime Minister – who always seemed to make up reality as he went along – with another issue important to John? Each decision was taken with consideration to all the others, and all taken with a view to moving the whole Labour Movement along.

Making sense of each addition, each judgment, was sometimes difficult. Why bother to listen to the bruised and fragile ego, why not attack a weak PM much more? If there was time, John would explain some of the dynamics, and if not he would bundle it together with other judgments for more discussions later on. He not only thought through why he was doing things, he would still ask for comments and advice.

Making Decisions

It is important to remember what an average day for the Leader of the Opposition is like. There are literally hundreds of decisions to be made – about very disparate activities. Some that are obviously concerned with future and important meaningful activity and others that look trivial and unimportant, but each one matters: each day fitted together into a network of seemingly unconnected actions, but really all constructed within an overall relationship. Nearly everything in politics impacted upon his work, and quite a lot of things outside of it. Making sense of all of it was John's skill.

That begins to explain some of the special strength that John had. He knew who he was with such clarity and certainty that he could really listen to others. He welcomed the fact that people around him had different ideas, and in fact made sure that he appointed people who were different from him. When John said to me, 'What do you *really* think about it?' he really wanted you to say what you believed and wanted to happen. John recognised that he needed 'difference' around him that was committed both in ensuring those differences were there and engaging honesty in debate. He knew that coming to a judgment needed candid controversy although he desperately wanted to sort out problems in a concensual manner. Decisions, ideas, activity and indeed the whole of politics revolves around the importance of dispute. Leaders must not only be intellectually capable of such debate, but they must have the strength to see private discussion as absolutely necessary. John, of course, always engaged in the discussion around the differences with a calm assurance.

It is this strength that people recognised, and saw it was at the core of his ability to work so clearly. That clarity came from his commitment to the people he wanted to serve and the practical policies that he wanted to put into effect. That commitment in itself was based upon his religious beliefs coupled with his understanding of social obligation. These gave him both the moral strength and also the day-to-day guidance to ensure that the *tactics* of each decision stemmed from an overall strategy.

John had a clear view of what he wanted to do, and what sort of society he wanted to be part of developing. He knew enough about the frailties of the human condition not be starry eyed about the future. But he had a commitment to ordinary men and women and their potential that was at times fierce. He would sometimes have a moment's hesitation about some of the 'tactics' necessary in the day-to-day hurly burly, and turn to me and ask if I thought he would be forgiven! Then he would go through why a particular action or decision was necessary in the overall scheme. His scheme was not just about leading the Labour Party; his scheme was about changing the opportunities for people in this country.

When John was elected as leader, there were those who thought that after a honeymoon period, he might have trouble with the Party. After all, he had never been on the National Executive, he had not been one of the 'fixers'. John set about tackling that part of the project. He knew that even though he had a Deputy with long experience of the party machine, he could not simply leave that aspect of responsibility to her. That would have fatally weakened his position. He caused much disquiet among some of the trade unionists on the Executive by refusing to tell them what he wanted them to do. He was acutely aware that because of the work done by Neil Kinnock before him, he was able to take a different approach. He would let people know what he was concerned about, but really did want them to think it through for themselves. He also made sure that he got around the country meeting the party members. He attended regional conferences. He wanted to encourage and give party members a sense of the commitment he had to the future, but he also wanted to feel the mood of the party, and assess the potential of the party members.

Fit to Govern

This was all done not to secure his position, but to secure the party for the changes necessary to win the election and make the Labour Party fit to govern for a generation. Leading the Labour Party was really something that I always knew John would be prepared to give up if he knew he was not succeeding in moving towards those longer-term goals. He was so self-assured that he really did not need the leadership for himself, but the leadership was for much more. John never deluded himself. He would not delude himself if things had started to go wrong. Precisely because he was at ease with himself, he didn't need to be continually reassured that all was well. He knew when he had not done well – and dealt with it.

This self-assurance could have come across as arrogance. It never did. He didn't need to parade it because, like his Christian conviction, it simply formed the base which made work possible. His commitment to public service and to social justice were reflected in many of the tributes to him. But that was his mission. He knew that things could be different, that the potential of ordinary people was being so wasted that it impoverished their lives, and the lives of those around him.

Working with John, the most remarkable thing was seeing how somehow he did manage to get the best out of us all. He expected us to work hard to be part of his determination to shift this country, to open up opportunities, to give people hope. I know that that was how he would have governed.

2

A Scottish Presbyterian

Having been a trade union official for twelve years, Norman Hogg was first elected to Parliament as MP for East Dunbartonshire defeating the Scottish Nationalists in 1979, and is now Member for Cumbernauld and Kilsyth. Having served as Labour's Scottish Whip and Deputy Chief Whip, he is Chair of Labour Friends of Israel. He is an Elder of the Church of Scotland and a Vice-President of the Christian Socialist Movementr.

Scottish Presbyterianism is a demanding doctrine. In this day much of its teaching and practice is lost to easy evangelism or fundamentalism or more usually both. John Smith subscribed to neither.

Scottish Presbyterianism requires commitment. It demands faith. It places the individual alone before God. There are no intermediaries except Christ himself. It recognises no hierarchy. There can be no great office holders. Bishops and priests have no place. The moderator or minister is but a first among equals recognised only for his learning, life and doctrine. The living Christ is head of the Church. Calvin's doctrine of the 'priesthood of all believers' insists on that commitment. Those who are counted for Christ must also be his advocates among the unbelievers.

The Scots' Experience

Such a strong doctrine has historically appealed to the Scots. It pitted them against the rigours of life. It required them to read and study. They could relate biblical truth to the experiences of a life often hard and conducted against great adversity. They exacted from the gentry a right to education. A school in every parish was Knox's ideal. The egalitarian idea was born. From the moment the Scottish reformers won that concession from a nervous aristocracy the Scots were on a very different road from their neighbours in Anglican England or Catholic Ireland. Politics had its Presbyterian dimension. In our day John Smith epitomised that.

Standing alone was no more easy for John Smith than it is for anyone else. He was a Party man. He once observed to me that one reason he was in the Labour Party was because he liked the way Labour did things. He approved of the way Labour arrived at its policy decisions. He could and did operate the apparatus of power inside the Labour Party, the Cabinet, the conference or wherever the Party found itself making decisions. He took the view that the quality of the decisions taken related to how sound they were when set against Labour's principles.

Labour's Philosophy

Christian Socialism has returned as the underlying philosophy of Labour in this day. John Smith had much to do with that but he would have readily admitted it was always there. The social manifesto of Christianity has always appealed to British socialists and drove socialist thinking in the formative years of British Labour.

John Smith never thought that there was a Marxist or other philosophical basis to the Labour Party other than Christian Socialism. Calvin and Knox may have stood behind him as they stand behind most Scottish Presbyterians but he was not their man either. The notion that John was a Calvinist would bring only a smile to the faces of those who knew and loved him. He had far too generous a view of his fellow human beings to embrace the cold doctrines of John Calvin or John Knox. But they were there in his political philosophy.

He may, in the words of Robert Burns, have 'gently scanned his fellow man' but that did not mean he was immediately understanding of their situation. He did tend to think that we were all as strong as himself which left some of us just a little overawed by him. But strictures, such as they were, never lasted. He was quick to point out the merits of individuals, particularly his MPs, who may earlier have fallen down on the job or in some other way.

His capacity to laugh, enjoy and participate in life to the full marked him out from other Scottish Presbyterians who are remembered for their stern and unbending view of the human condition. John Smith was no John Reith or Stafford Cripps. They would have commanded his respect. Respect for John Smith was won by other qualities that were entirely his own.

The Right Thing

John Smith saw Christianity as demanding of its adherents and followers to do the right thing simply because it *was* the right thing. This bull point was at the heart of his lecture to the Christian Socialist Movement in March 1993.

He laid great importance on that R H Tawney memorial lecture he gave in the Bloomsbury Central Baptist Church. His staff were left in no doubt that he saw the event as crucially important. It was to set out his very own view of what he and his leadership of a great political party were all about. This was no address to the Party faithful. There would not be a demonstrative audience at a Party rally. This had to be a thought-through prospectus that the audience would recognise as the real thing. It was a speech that later in the same year would be compared with the 'Back to Basics' speech of the Prime Minister and all that subsequently flowed from that. John Smith's lecture had depth designed to provoke a thoughtful Christian analysis of the prevailing political condition. He offered a new moral agenda that was to become the cornerstone of Labour Party thinking as it approaches the next general election. Labour was to occupy the moral high ground.

His attack on the New Right of the 1980s exposed their adulation of the individual and emphasis on self. He spoke of the value of community and rounded on the failures of Thatcherism. He asserted that the people had never embraced the dogmas of Thatcherism and that a society organised on the basis of concern for others was the only possible basis for a civilised society.

John Smith knew that the Left in politics is and must be optimistic. It sees the best in people. It looks for the noble in human endeavour. It believes that society achieves its best when it inspires the best in human beings. He enjoined Christian Socialists to optimism. They should, he said, be optimistic because there is so much good that can be done if we seize the opportunities. His only concession to caution was to add that that there is so much that needs to be done.

He did not dress up his Christianity into some obscure incomprehensible doctrine that left out any opportunity to question the validity of his views or policies. He had the clarity and the transparency that went with the highly territorial variety of his Protestant Christianity. It became the hallmark of the man.

It was because his life was so effectively rooted in his Christianity that he was an effective politician and statesman.

A Clear Mind

He always had a clear and unambiguous mind on every issue that arose. He was never defeated by events. He never despaired of events. He took the view that he was in the business of addressing events and problems. There could be no running away from difficulties and decision-making. There was a Party to be led and people out there looking for answers. They maybe included many for whom answers provided hope for the future. Others were maybe sceptical or cynical. He understood that. People were always entitled to respect. John Smith was never cynical when it came to people. His was the responsibility to state where Labour stood, and it had to stand up. The people would soon rumble a fudge. When in the 1992 general election he unfurled Labour's policies for taxation his action had the great merit of honesty. He could not, and it would not have ever occurred to him to, do anything less than explain the facts of Labour's intentions. Knowing that he had acted in accordance with the standards he set for his own public life he was able to round on the Tory Government in 1993 and 1994 when their actions on taxation were exposed.

Sectarianism

During the conduct of the 1994 by-election in his former constituency in Monklands East, there arose questions about the religious sectarianism unfortunately evident among the people and endemic in Lanarkshire. It was suggested that John Smith had avoided the issue and that his apparent silence amounted to an acceptance of the situation.

Nothing could be further from the truth. He was deeply conscious that religious sectarianism existed and very much aware of its causes and consequences. He ignored attempts by political opponents, mainly Tory back-benchers now largely discredited, to exploit the situation. He was unimpressed by the conduct of Monklands District Council but recognised, as only a Queen's Counsel could, that action followed only upon receiving substantiated evidence. He challenged those who offered claims of discrimination, corruption and financial malpractice to produce their evidence and more significantly demanded that the Secretary of State for Scotland conduct a public enquiry. The latter declined. The former preferred the political advantage of smears to righting a wrong.

None the less, religious intolerance and sectarianism are factors in the life of a community where historically it was convenient to have scapegoats to explain the hard and appalling conditions of the Scotland that emerged with the Industrial Revolution.

Throughout his constituency, elsewhere in Lanarkshire and in the neighbouring constituencies, there exist villages where the population are all or predominantly of one religion. This is no accident, although the house-letting policies of Labour-controlled local authorities have sought to redress this situation.

Historically the bosses, whether coal owners or iron masters, segregated the people. They capitalised on the strong feelings engendered by Irish immigration. The all too familiar arguments were deployed that the 'incomers' were taking jobs, would work for less than the going rate and accept poor conditions. These were diversions that distracted attention from the real issues surrounding the working and social conditions that prevailed. If the workers were arguing about religion they were less likely to argue with their employers about wages.

The trade unions and the Labour Party would have none of this. To the lasting credit of the movement its members were treated simply as members, whether Catholic or Protestant. This gave Catholic Irish immigrants their best opportunity for emancipation in local communities. They took it and throughout this century, which has seen the ascendancy of the Labour Party in Scotland, Catholics have played and continue to play leading roles in equal partnership with Protestants, Jews, Moslems and non-believers.

The Labour movement practised its egalitarian principles while organised religion fostered sectarianism or at best failed to address it. They denied St Paul's edict that in Christ Jesus there is neither Jew nor Greek. Today in industrial Scotland the churches of all denominations are declining.

Today also fewer and fewer march in Orange parades. The Orange Order has little appeal to young people. Religious intolerance should have no place in contemporary Scotland. It is to be hoped that in the 1994 Monklands East by-election naked sectarianism has made its last throw.

Tackling Intolerance

John Smith despised intolerance but recognised that it could not be tackled head on but rather by patient argument, example, education and righting the social wrongs on which such ugly doctrines feed. He saw in the Labour Party the most effective vehicle for achieving these goals – a practical machinery for the advancement of Christian Socialism.

He understood the Labour Party and how it worked. He was comfortable with it and the people in it. He had an uncomplicated view of its role and purpose. He deplored its schisms which he saw as a betrayal of those it sought to represent. He was furious when, at the height of defections to the deservedly ill-fated Social Democratic Party, a member of his General Management Committee congratulated him on remaining in the Labour Party. The GMC delegate did not know John Smith. He certainly knew him after he had replied to the insult! He was disparaging of those who reneged and left Labour at that time. He campaigned to save the Labour Party, addressing meetings that were often hostile. He displayed great courage and leadership while others scuttled away to political obscurity.

The Trade Unions

If the Labour Party is a machine for practical politics then so too is the trade union movement. Victor Feather once described the TUC as a 'nuts and bolts organisation'.

John Smith's Christian socialist values were set out in his speech to the Trades Union Congress on September 7th, 1993. That speech marked a cementing of the traditional, if sometimes strained, relationship with the Labour Party. He said: 'As the people of this country turn away from a discredited and decaying government, it is our responsibility – our shared responsibility – to show them a new way forward.'

Asserting the relationship is not and was not in any way novel or new. It is something every Labour leader says when addressing the annual congress of the TUC. What was different was that the modernising drive currently motivating the Labour leadership included the trade unions.

Fashionable as it was to suggest that Labour was jettisoning the unions, it was never John Smith's view. He saw trade unions as a continuing component of the Labour Party, but also as part of the engine of change that would rebuild Britain in the post-Tory years when he hoped to lead a new Labour government.

He was proud of being a trade unionist. Queen's Counsels and eminent members of the Scottish Bar are not noted for their trade union allegiances but John Smith was the exception. He liked being the butt of Commons Tearoom jokes that he was a boilermaker. He was a member of the boilermakers' union before it merged with the General and Municipal Workers to become the GMB. He was sponsored first by the Boilermakers and later by its successor. He saw the value of trade unionism, its principles and its practical nuts and bolts work for work-people and their families.

If his commitment was clear then so too was his right as a Labour leader and participating trade unionist to say where he thought the movement should go. He could not have been clearer as to how its principles should be expressed in the exercise of power within the decision-making of the Labour Party. That may have offended some trade union leaders, but those of us who knew him were never in any doubt that if he had not won the battle for 'One Member One Vote' (OMOV) he would have quit the leadership.

In the summer of 1993, over tea one afternoon in the House of Commons Smoking Room, he made plain to me his intention to quit if the vote went the wrong way. The knowledge of his intentions worried me through the run-up to the Party's annual conference at Brighton. I knew he meant what he said. The principle at stake was fundamental to his whole political philosophy, his Christian commitment and his foundation in Presbyterian practice. The day of fudge was over. There were those who should have known that when he was elected. The form of words, the shabby compromise designed to please everybody in the conference hall were never likely to please him. He had to succeed. It had to be right.

I knew John Smith for over thirty-five years. I was never in any doubt that the man was special. He was tough in a tough profession. He was intellectually robust. He was principled at a time when party politics and politicians of all persuasions found pragmatism an easier route to follow. His leadership was discharged with an authority that led to universal respect.

The Labour Party knew before he became leader that he had all the qualities required for the job. He was an all but unanimous choice for the office. That gave him added authority but never did he seek to be authoritarian. Even in the dark days of the OMOV row he sought to out-argue rather than out-organise or out-manoeuvre his opponents. It was his style to win the argument by the strength of his case and the quality of his advocacy. The smoke-filled room belonged to another day and very different leaders.

A cruel blow was struck at the nation and the Labour movement when John Smith died. But he left both the country and the Party the richer for his having been with us. His legacy will be fulfilled when a new Labour government is elected on policies to which he gave a new moral basis – policies that express the vision of Christian Socialism.

3

How Beautiful Upon the Mountains

Chris Smith was educated at George Watson's College in Edinburgh and Pembroke College, Cambridge. He worked as a housing specialist, and was an Islington councillor from 1978 to 1983. He was elected MP for Islington South and Finsbury in 1983, and served in John Smith's Shadow Treasury team from 1987 to 1992. Since 1992 he has been Labour's Shadow Secretary of State for the Environment covering Environmental Protection. He is a Director of Sadler's Wells Theatre, and a Vice-President and Trustee of the Christian Socialist Movement.

My fondest and clearest memory of John Smith is not of his forensic wit at the Dispatch Box in the House of Commons, or even of the common-sense way in which he could cut through a meandering discussion in the Shadow Cabinet, splendid though he was in both settings. It is of standing at the summit of Fionn Bheinn with him, in the far north-west of Scotland, just five short weeks before he died.

It had been a hard struggle to get there. The wind had been whipping squalls of snow across, the cloud had come and gone, we'd had to put on our crampons to tackle the final five hundred feet, and for a moment just short of the summit we'd been completely enveloped in a thick mist with no sense of ground or sky at all. But when we finally arrived at the top, the cloud lifted, and we could see for miles across the snowswept hills of Torridon. John looked and felt on top of the world.

John Smith loved the Scottish hills. I can remember so well the days we spent together in the mountains. The time on the South Cluanie Ridge under a scorching sun when we could see the whole western seaboard of Scotland. The descent from Beinn Dearg near Ullapool, done at double-quick pace because there was a meal and a dram waiting at the end. Or the burst of applause that greeted us on a summit above Glencoe when the Shadow Chancellor – as he then was – arrived at the cairn (being filmed all the while by ITN) to find a crowd of walkers already there and determined to show that he was welcome.

A Steady Climb

He would treat his mountains with respect, taking the ascent slowly and steadily, but always getting there in the end. It was a bit of a metaphor for his political life, in a way: not rushing anything, but being very clear about the objective, and always succeeding in attaining it. After his first heart attack, he had set himself the task of climbing all the 3,000-foot mountains in Scotland, called the 'Munros' after a crusty old Victorian Tory, Sir Hugh Munro, who first tabulated them all. There are 277 of them, and since 1988 John had completed 108. It was no mean feat, given the intense pressures on him both as Shadow Chancellor and as Leader of the Opposition. But he had given himself a goal, and he was determined to achieve it. The wall of his office at the Commons had a map of the Munros on it, with pins stuck in to indicate where his conquests had been. It was a constant reminder and spur to further endeavour.

One of the reasons for his hillwalking was, quite simply, that he enjoyed it. Sometimes of course the effort was frustrating. I was with him on his final mountain, near Ullapool, and the soft deep snow that cloaked the top half of the hill made every step feel as if we were wading through treacle. On another occasion, heading for the summit of Bynack More in the Cairngorms, the horizontal hail that forced us to bend almost double eventually imposed the judicious decision on us to turn back rather than struggle on. But despite the effort and the weather and the difficulties he liked the exercise and the fresh air and the views. He also revelled in the company. He could be an enormously entertaining companion for a day on the hill. On our final walk together we put the British economy to rights; we speculated on who would be the next Chairman of the Conservative Party; we talked about everything from the environment to education policy; and John reminisced about his student days making tea on a 'puffer' going up and down the west coast of Scotland.

A Spiritual Approach

As well as the enjoyment, the exercise and the company, however, there was something more spiritual about his approach to the mountains. 'I will lift up mine eyes unto the hills; from whence cometh my help' (Psalm 121, KJV). He found in the wild and empty hill landscapes, I believe, a touch of the divine. It's a deeply romantic appreciation of the natural world, a Coleridgian sense of the infinite present in

21

the finite world around us. John shared in this, though in his down-to-earth way he would never have put it quite like that. He was never one for purple prose about what he saw around him on his walks, but he sensed that somehow these ranges of hills and folded glens could stand as waymarks for something deeper and more eternal than simple material beauty.

It was particularly fitting that Gerard Manley Hopkins' poem 'Inversnaid' was read so movingly at John's memorial service in Westminster Abbey.

> What would the world be, once bereft
> Of wet and of wildness? Let them be left,
> O let them be left, wildness and wet;
> Long live the weeds and the wilderness yet.

Hopkins' poem celebrates the sheer physical force of the water and the landscape, conveys to us its colour and texture and material reality, but then carries us into the deeper perception of the spiritual values it imparts to the human heart. He never said it to me, but I am sure that John felt the same when he listened to the roaring water of a highland stream in a sunlit glen at the end of a hard day's walk.

There were practical, political lessons to be learned from his love of hillwalking, too. I well remember that just a few days before he died I had brought an environment policy paper to a Party committee chaired by John. Amongst its proposals was something that people have campaigned for for over a hundred years: giving the ordinary people of Britain a right to roam over open country, mountain and moorland. It's something I dearly hope will be enthusiastically passed into law by a Labour government. John commented drily: 'This is something I have a vested interest in.' He endorsed the idea instantly.

Reflecting Contrasts

This linking of the practical with the spiritual – something that characterised John's life and politics – is a thoroughly Scottish trait. It's what Gregory Smith, many decades ago, called the Caledonian Antisyzygy – a term almost deliberately abstruse in its pedantry. He meant the way in which Scottish life and literature reflect contrasts, seek to combine opposites, to have on the one hand a sense of detail, a realism, an intimacy of style, yet on the other to be able to embrace a fantasy world, full of fun and wonder and difference. Scottish literature is shot through with these contrasts between finely-honed detail and broadly-sweeping fancy. John's ability to puncture windy pomposity with an earthy realism, yet his simultaneous capacity to be deeply moved by things beyond the material, demonstrated precisely the same combination of opposites. Climbing mountains brought him both experiences.

If John found a sense of the infinite within the natural world around him, he found the same sense of limitless possibility in the lives of his fellow citizens. He used to speak with passion about the need to unlock the extraordinary potential of ordinary people. He detested poverty and oppression and inequality, not just because it generated human misery and rendered people powerless, but also because it wasted talent. It meant that people were denied the opportunity to develop their full potential, to make the contribution to society that they could. It is why he used to speak constantly about his ambition to make Britain the best-educated and best-trained nation in Europe. Education was the key to developing potential, to enabling people to thrive in their own way and to the full limit of their own capacities.

One of the most profound of John Keats' letters, written

in 1819, speaks of how misguided is the traditional conception of the world as a 'vale of tears', and continues:

> Call the world if you Please 'The vale of Soul-making'. Then you will find the use of the world . . . I say 'Soul-making' Soul as distinguished from an Intelligence – There may be intelligences or sparks of divinity in millions – but they are not Souls till they acquire identities, till each one is personally itself . . . How then are Souls to be made? How then are these sparks which are God to have identity given them . . . How, but by the medium of a world like this?

> John Keats, Letter to George and Georgiana Keats,
> Sunday 14th February – Monday 3rd May 1819

I have no idea if John ever read this remarkable insight from Keats, but the schooling of a spark of divinity into an identity or soul might stand as a spiritual metaphor for precisely that drawing-out of individual talent into fulfilment that he saw as one of the principal goals of public policy.

Pathways out of Poverty

It was not only in the field of education and training that he felt this need. He knew about the sheer hopelessness and frustration and fatalism that sets in when poverty and unemployment blight someone's life. He coined the phrase 'pathways out of poverty' to describe the ambition he felt ought to invest the benefit system, and felt real anger when Tories tried to dismiss those on Income Support or Invalidity or Unemployment Benefit as somehow entering a culture of dependency. He wanted the financial safety-net of the welfare state to be there as a help for people to rise, rather than as a trap to hold them back. When the Conservative Chancellor simultaneously raised National Insurance contributions and cut the benefits people received he attacked the decision with a genuinely indignant anger that made his immediate Budget Day response – one of the most difficult speeches any Opposition Leader ever has to make – a model of its kind. It was good precisely because it stemmed from a real and abiding passion about the sheer waste of poverty and unemployment. The innate potential of people was being held back, and for John that was something that diminished all of us.

These same values that infused John's politics – and his approach to the hills too – must now be carried forward by the rest of us as we aim for government. There is so much we need to learn from him. First, and perhaps most obviously, an appreciation of the need to conserve the beauty of the natural world, and to ensure that its enjoyment is open to all and not just to the privileged few. John had long been intending, for example, to visit Creag Meghaidh beside Loch Laggan, to see at first hand the work which the Scottish Natural Heritage have been accomplishing in the regeneration of original woodland and habitat. He wanted to bag a peak or two at the same time, of course; but he was keen to see the pioneering conservation work that has been developed there.

Open Access

The sharing of the enjoyment of nature with all went without question for him. The fact that the Duke of Westminster, who owns the Forest of Bowland in Lancashire, could prohibit access to ordinary people over most of his land for most of the year, was something John could never accept. In most of Scotland there has for many years been a tradition of permitted access, although there are some instances now of this breaking down, and there can be severe problems in the stalking season. The most recent attempts of the government to introduce a new offence of aggravated trespass, even in Scotland, enraged him. A new Act under a Labour government, sweeping away aggravated trespass and enshrining a right of access to open country, mountain and moorland, will be one of the best memorials we can institute for John Smith.

We must hold fast, too, to his passion for social justice. His understanding of the struggles faced by those who are not rich or privileged or successful – drawn from his own Ardrishaig background, and from his work amongst his constituents in Airdrie and Coatbridge, and from his deep personal convictions – led him to a firm commitment to use the power of government to provide opportunity for those to whom it is denied. His commitment to education and training formed part of that understanding. So did his firm belief in the need for a national minimum wage; this, too, will be a fitting legislative memorial. John could list the intellectual arguments for a statutory minimum wage as well as any: the comparison with the situation in other countries; the fact that it would add only 1 per cent to the overall national wages bill; the way in which supposed safety-net schemes like Family Credit are not reaching those they were purported to be designed for. But his attachment to the concept derived above all from a burning realisation that it quite simply cannot be right for an employer to pay a pittance for a good job of work. And if the power of government can be used to intervene to prevent this happening, then he felt it was a moral duty for government to do so.

Moral Duty

The concept of moral duty for government sits very oddly in these cynical political times, in the dog days of the Tory years here in Britain. But John Smith personified perhaps more than any other contemporary politician this sense of duty, and it is perhaps this, in part, which led to the remarkable national outpouring of grief at his passing. With John, you always knew that – deep down – there was a fundamental core of belief that would never waver or be discarded. In all the turmoil over the formation of the Social Democrats and the departure of senior figures from the Labour Party, John never even thought about leaving. He believed so firmly in the Party's core commitment to the needs of ordinary people, and in the duty of government to bear that goal ever in mind, that he could never even entertain the possibility of departing from his allegiance.

Someone recently characterised the difference between the two main parties to me thus: if you had asked an average voter twenty years ago what the difference was, he said, they would have told us that the Tory Party stood for the rich and privileged and wealthy and the establishment, whilst the Labour Party stood for the rest – and the rest included me, the ordinary citizen. Nowadays, he said, they would have replied that the Labour Party stood for the poor and the disadvantaged and the ill and the elderly, and the Tory Party stood for the rest – and the rest included me, the ordinary citizen. This is a crude shorthand for a complex argument, but it is none the less telling. The Labour Party cannot possibly lose its innate commitment to the very poorest and most vulnerable in our society. If we lose that, we become as nothing. Almost our whole *raison d'etre* disappears. But at the same time we mustn't allow the rest of the electorate to think that we are exclusively engaged upon an exercise on behalf of the poor. Embracing both within our message is what is important.

John Smith understood this very well. He felt real and passionate anger about the treatment of those least able to fend for themselves. It was anger that exploded at Budget time, when it shone through everything he said. But it affected other aspects as well. He hated the Social Fund – dreamed up by John Major when he was a junior Social Security Minister, and almost deliberately designed to patronise the very poor. He had been outraged by the government's hamfisted attempts to scupper a Bill to give real rights to people with disabilities. Yet at the same time as he felt and expressed all of these things, he did so in a way which included the rest of society as well.

Building Bridges

Building bridges in order to make progress was John's particular skill. In the old debate between 'modernisers' and 'traditionalists' he would have proudly proclaimed himself as both, seeing both approaches as having something to offer to the Party. He combined both in his own persona, and certainly for the period of his own leadership, he rendered the distinction more or less irrelevant. We must aim to do the same. He combined a firm attachment to some very traditional values of fairness with a thoroughly modern recognition of how to appeal successfully to a modern audience. And he united the entire Party in doing so.

This is a legacy we must not throw away. When confronted by what is sometimes called the one-third two-thirds society, some people might argue that the one-third should effectively be abandoned in the search for a majority. Not

John. Precisely because of that fundamental belief in the extraordinary potential within ordinary people, he wanted to see all parts of society and their needs taken into account. It would not only be inhuman but would be a waste to do anything else. When addressing, intensively if necessary, the needs of the one-third, the aspirations of the two-thirds should not be ignored.

The Individual in Society

To John, there always *was* such a thing as society. He knew, more deeply perhaps than most in the Party, that the true fulfilment of the individual citizen can only be achieved in the context of a strong and supportive community: that the needs of the person and the wellbeing of society are totally and utterly interdependent. There are many different ways of defining socialism, probably almost as many as there are people trying to define it. Some elements of the British democratic socialist tradition are clear: the striving for equality between classes; the desire to achieve things for all, not just for the few; the recognition of the value of labour in the industrial process; the campaign for enhanced democracy. But perhaps most important of all, there is a sense of the interrelationship between the individual and the community of which we are all part, the sense that if we do things together, we will do them better and more effectively. And that you cannot achieve everything by acting on your own, as an isolated individual.

Nowhere perhaps is this more true than in relation to the protection of our environment. You cannot privatise the ozone layer. You cannot buy or sell a piece of air (though I have a suspicion the Tories would like to try if they could find a way to do it). You need to take common decisions, in a shared way, in order to take collective responsibility for the environment around us. The free market never ever protected anyone's environment. Bureaucratic state centralism as practised in Eastern Europe and the Soviet Union didn't do a particularly good job, either. The key components for a sensible environment policy are community, democracy and equity. And if anyone is looking for a three-word definition of today's socialism, then they could do a lot worse than that.

The Conservation of Beauty

Let us apply these lessons, therefore, to the protection of the wildest and most important parts of the Scottish Highlands which John Smith so loved. The conservation of beauty is something to be valued and sought as a common goal. It cannot be done by giving a series of private landowners a free rein to do as they please with land they happen to own. (It has always seemed to me inherently absurd that someone can 'own' a mountain.) It has to be done by a judicious use of governmental power, planning restrictions on inappropriate uses or developments, incentives and assistance for particular conservation objectives, and rights and responsibilities for other citizens. When government sits back and does nothing – as it has done in the cases of both Mar Lodge and Glen Feshie, areas of the utmost landscape importance in the Cairngorms – then a spiral of decline can set in. John would have strongly argued that there was a moral duty on government to take action – on behalf of society as a whole – to preserve the most precious and important parts of our natural heritage.

The spiritual uplift from the hills; the divine spark in the ordinary individual; the need to fight for the dignity of that individual; and the recognition that a strong community, an active government, are required in order to achieve it: these are John Smith's values that we must carry with us into the future. How fitting it is that John should have been buried on Iona, the resting place of Scottish kings and the landing place of St Columba, a place of intense natural beauty and one where the physical world is infused with a sense of the spiritual. Towards the end of T. S. Eliot's *Murder in the Cathedral*, the Chorus of the Women of Canterbury touch a particularly resonant chord:

> For wherever a saint has dwelt, wherever a martyr has
>   given his blood for the blood of Christ,
> There is holy ground, and the sanctity shall not depart
>   from it
> Though armies trample over it, though sightseers come
>   with guide-books looking over it;
> From where the western seas gnaw at the coast of Iona,
> To the death in the desert, the prayer in forgotten places
>   by the broken imperial column,
> From such ground springs that which forever renews
>   the earth
>   Though it is forever denied.

Collected Plays (Faber and Faber, London, 1962), pp. 53–4

4

The Modern Right to Freedom

Baroness Dean of Thornton-le-Fylde was previously General Secretary of the printing union SOGAT during the Wapping dispute, and is now one of Labour's members of the House of Lords. She is Chair of the Trustees of the Christian Socialist Movement. She is also Chair of ICSTIS (the Independent Committee for the Supervision of Television and Information Services), and is a member of the Armed Forces Pay Review Body.

In *The Rights of Man* published as Europe was convulsed by the industrial and political revolutions of 200 years ago, Thomas Paine argued that 'Man did not enter into society to become worse than he was before, nor to have fewer rights than he had before, but to have those rights better secured.'[1] It is a depressing truth that here we are, all those years later and on the brink of a new century, still arguing the same case.

And in a way, what Tom Paine said then could have provided the text for John Smith's speech to the Trades Union Congress in 1993. It was a brave speech, his first and tragically, also his last to the TUC; he was witty, relaxed, and confident. It was an important speech and that gave his words an animation which touched a nerve in his audience. It was the speech of a leader, but it also reflected the thoughts of a man talking about issues he understood to people who understood him. It was also the speech of a man who knew where he stood and why, and that was recognised and admired by the trade unionists there in Brighton – as it would have been at any time in the course of the history of trade unionism.

John Smith himself made the point that the trade unions are no less needed today than they were at the first Congress in Manchester in 1868 – despite the progress we have made in the march of history.

Working Changes

There have been unimaginable advances since the turmoil of the late eighteenth century and the Industrial Revolution of the nineteenth. Yet the revolution we face in working practices today, the changes that it is necessary for our society to absorb in order to operate efficiently, provide at least as great a challenge as probably at any time in the last 200 years.

We have to examine how to manage the trend towards different work patterns which have emerged and will continue. The trend towards more part-time working; how to help those who have more than one job because the traditional full-time work is being broken down, or who are obliged to have more than one by the exigencies of current employment; how to protect women workers whose vulnerability is so readily exploited by the ruthless; how to handle changes in the family and the social structure – with the breakdown of traditional family patterns, a huge reduction in the number of so-called 'nuclear' families of two parents and two children and the emergence of new priorities for the working population which we can already see are being recognised far too late by the cumbersome structures of authority; all of this in a multi-cultural society in a ferment of advance.

These are challenges which will need to be addressed by the next Labour government, but in the meantime we still have to assess how to handle them until the present weary, worn-out government releases its now fragile hold on power. We cannot afford to wait.

Despite the leaps that the trade unions have made across the last century, it has still been possible for the present Conservative government to set back in a relatively short time the rate of progress – and in a manner that none of us would have thought possible in the 1960s and 1970s. They haven't exactly licensed children to go up chimneys again, but they have removed so many controls on employers and abandoned so much protection for employees that they have effectively reduced the rights of the individual at work.

The Right to Organise

And there is a moral right here, one which underpinned the whole of John Smith's thinking and which is what has always given trade unions their authority in society: it is the right of an individual to organise collectively to protect himself or herself if he or she wishes; the right to join a trade union; the right of unions to represent their membership. That simple fundamental right of trade union membership within our evolving modern society is a cornerstone of the dignity of working people and one that has been unceremoniously pushed aside by dogmatic Conservative governments.

It is the need for society to defend the rights of the individual that is one of the basic tenets of trade unionism. It also imbues the approach of those with a Christian faith. John Smith's attitude to employment, the world of work, the needs of the individual, was a combination of his belief both in trade unions and in Christianity, and it gave his message a simplicity that was recognised by everybody. The Tories may throw up their hands at the concept of a minimum wage; John Smith gave his commitment to it at the TUC in 1993, not because he was seeking easy, cheap popularity, but because he recognised that such a thing is necessary in order to defend every individual, particularly the weak and even those who do not have the industrial muscle of a trade union to defend them.

Take another echo from the history of trade unionism. Dorothy Thompson in *The Chartists* recalls Mr Rushton, a Chartist preacher, who used as a text 'The poor ye have always with you.' Mr Rushton apparently used to argue that there were three types of poor:

> There were God's poor, the maim and blind; there were the poor made so by reckless living, and who had put themselves in that position by their own actions; there were the poor who, despite having worked hard all their lives had been made poor or kept poor because of oppressive actions by others who had deprived them of their God-given rights.[2]

Rushton argued that it was a sin that some people lorded over others in an unjust way and that the misery of the poor resulted from the actions of the rich and powerful.

I quote from the past, but only to put into context

the essence of John Smith's approach: his basic recognition of the need always to learn, and to use what one had learned in order to go forward. He looked ahead. That was what he was like, the sort of man he was, pragmatic and practical, but his approach had everything to do with his sense of personal morality and political ethics.

In his essay in *Reclaiming the Ground*, John Smith, in paying tribute to R. H. Tawney, drew on the Christian faith which provided the foundation for Tawney's arguments, as it did for him too. John wrote:

> But he [Tawney] did not claim – nor should any Christian – that only Christianity could provide the moral framework for an ethical approach to politics. Our own experience tells us that an ethical approach to life and politics can be held as firmly by people of other faiths and by those who hold no religious conviction. Nor should Christian socialists ever seek to suggest that Christians must be socialists.[3]

That being said, as Smith himself went on to acknowledge, he held a profound conviction that politics ought to be a moral activity. The move to introduce 'One Member One Vote' for elections within the Labour Party, for example – a move I personally supported – arose partly from his fundamental belief that this was as much a moral issue as it was an assertion of the rights of the individual. The tension over the debate on this question at the 1993 Labour Conference was considerable and one reason was because John Smith saw its acceptance as vital for the whole future of the Labour Party. Everyone who knew him at all realised how keenly he felt about the outcome.

How ironic that its first use should be to select John's successor.

The Value of Society

It was not just a matter of what *he* thought, however; he also cared about what people thought of us and of leadership. He saw in our society, distorted as it so often is by greed and consumerism, the growing desire for more principle in politics. John wrote: 'I believe the tide of opinion is beginning to flow towards a recognition of the value of society and away from the nihilistic individualism of so much of modern Conservatism.'

Margaret Thatcher, of course, famously once asserted that there was 'no such thing as society' (a statement from which she attempted later to retreat, but which still amply illustrated her way of thinking) and it was small wonder that she was on a collision course with the Church from the very beginning of her period as Prime Minister.

She also once complained, in one of those clever phrases put into her mouth by her speech-writers, about attempts to introduce socialism in Britain 'by the back Delors'. What it boiled down to was that she did not want to accept the kind of changes that would be expected of us by the social chapter requirements for increasing European cohesion for a number of simple reasons. John Smith referred to them in his TUC speech too. He called it a national humiliation. He said:

British workers work the longest hours in Europe. We have the worst employment protection laws. We are the only EC country where there is no legal right to paid annual holidays. The gap between the pay of male and female manual workers in Britain is the worst in Europe.

Britain as we know is the only country in Europe which offers its workers no protection against low pay.

And has all this been in order to effect some extraordinary economic miracle in Britain? On the contrary.

The Second Tory Recession

We are now, it is hoped, experiencing the beginning of the end of the second major economic recession in the course of over fifteen years of Tory government – this, of course, from the party that is supposed to be able to manage the economy. But even if an economic upturn is now under way at last, it is not an experience that is being received with undiluted joy by those facing continual grinding poverty, the homeless and the unemployed.

We do not really know how many jobs have been sacrificed to the costly economic experiments that the Conservatives have been conducting with our industry, our manufacturing base, our children's hopes, our national pride. That is because they have consistently changed the manner of assessing how they count the victims of their unsuccessful economic management. Even by their reckoning, however, we do know that there have been over two million people without jobs for every month of at least twelve years of the Tory term in office.

Different people have different prescriptions for what to do about this. We are suffering from decades of poor investment in education and training, in industry and in research. Common sense dictates that in order to manage the current uneasy economic situation and to provide the prospect of social cohesion for the future this must be redressed. But how? There are several ways of answering that question, but I have no doubt that whatever economic solution is applied it must be forward-looking in a number of ways. Firstly we must recognise the changes in our society, the continuing changes in the nature and structure of work and how that impacts on people, and of course changes in the structure of our families.

As a trade unionist and one who shares this view of the moral basis of political activity, my answer is that we have to do more to protect all our futures and the way to achieve this is partly through investment. The capitalist answer would invest for the greater benefit of the shareholder; but I believe that a truly moral approach is to invest in the people: in training, in giving people the skills they need and thus giving people the ability to lift themselves from poverty, to support their families and contribute to society.

Human Freedom

By this means you offer people real choices, real freedom, real individual rights. That is something that was recognised in the recent Roman Catholic document *Centesimus Annus*. It said, 'Economic freedom is only one element of human freedom. When it becomes autonomous, when man is seen more as a producer or consumer of goods than as a subject who produces and consumes in order to live, then economic freedom loses its necessary relationship to the human person and ends up alienating and oppressing him.'

That extract was quoted recently by the Archbishop of Canterbury, Dr George Carey, in a speech to the Christian Association of Business Executives in June 1994, in which he laid down the precept that a society which allows principles to guide action is more likely to be – dare one make the reference? – a nation at ease with itself. Dr Carey reminded his audience, in an address he entitled 'The Mission of Business' that God created human beings with distinctive skills, powers of memory and ingenuity. He went on:

> Our ability to apply those distinctive skills to natural resources, to create things of use and value to ourselves and others is God-given, part of his creation. Moreover, it is inherent in the commandment to love our neighbour as ourselves that we will use our skills, among other things, to fashion from the world's resources new products which bring joy, comfort, protection, delights and edification to our fellow human beings.

He was speaking of what R. H. Tawney once called 'the extraordinary potential of ordinary people'. That was something John Smith believed in, too. But he also recognised that it was something that we all, as members of the same society, had to be careful to ensure was not abused by the unscrupulous. That was what made him a Christian and a socialist. In the Labour Party and the trade unions we must all be alert to the continuing need to protect the weak, but we also have to look to the future and how best to use our strength. As individuals we can see the potential that can be achieved through our membership of a political party and of a proud trade union movement. It is not enough, however, to look back to our history of achievement across the last century, which has seen so much industrial and political advance. We have to look ahead. We have to repair the damage of the Tories' years in office. We have to restore our right to play our part in society as members of trade unions or political parties, freely expressing once again the choices that have been eroded in the recent past. Given those rights, we have then to demonstrate that we accept the responsibilities

they impose upon us. That must surely be the mark of a truly
free society.

BIBLIOGRAPHICAL NOTES

1 Thomas Paine, *Political Writings*, ed. Bruce Kuklick (CUP, Cambridge,
1989).
2 D. Thompson, *The Chartists* (Temple Smith, London 1984).
3 John Smith, *Reclaiming the Ground* (Spire, London, 1993).

5

Social Justice: Waste and Promise

John Battle first came into political life through Church Action on Poverty, of which he was the first National Co-ordinator, and through Leeds City Council, where he was Chair of Housing. He was elected as MP for Leeds West in 1987, and is Shadow Minister for Housing. He is a Trustee of the Christian Socialist Movement.

The present world situation requires of the Christian a new vision and praxis of the message of Christ as an effective announcement of hope and love; that is to say, a deep and keen consciousness of the tremendous injustices perpetrated today in the economic, social, political and international fields; a frank attitude of denouncing the structures of oppression; an effective act of commitment for the integral liberation of everyone; an honest acknowledgement of our silence, even of our identification with the socio-economic structures that oppress the poor and marginalised.

Juan Alfaro SJ　　*Theology of Justice in the World*

Women living in the favellas, the inner-city shanty towns, of

Sao Paulo, Brazil, were literally building a new community
on land given to them on the outskirts by the city council.
The costs of breeze blocks and timber were pooled. The
labour was shared. Already a radio station, a community
centre, and church, some shops and a training base had
gone up amidst the house building. They referred to it as
their *mutirao* project. No one could find an English synonym
for this word; 'community building' or 'mutual help' were
too limited. Someone suggested the Gaelic word *methel* as
the nearest equivalent. Rooted in an agricultural setting, it
apparently refers to seeing the storm blowing up in the sky
with your own harvest in, though your neighbour's is not,
and without a word, or a contract, all going to harvest your
neighbours's field before the wind and rain come to ruin
it. You do it, knowing that in a few weeks' time you will
be competing for a price to sell your harvest in the same
market-place. You do it because the needs of the people as
a whole take precedence over the market price.

Beyond the Market

The Labour Party leader John Smith always emphasised that
there was something more basic than markets. Challenging
recent interpretations of Adam Smith and neo-liberal economists, he wrote

> the truth, of course is that markets are social institutions
> created within communities that have already developed
> complex structures of co-operation and common iden-
> tity: structures which have been characteristic features
> of human existence since the earliest days of civilisation
> . . . and it is within these civil institutions, held together
> by bonds of mutual trust and consent – absolutely crucial

elements of human co-operation – that the business of markets is able to take place at all.[1]

There would have been an English synonym for *mutirao* that may have been lost in the Industrial Revolution. The development in John Smith's work of the concept of social justice, so predominant in his efforts as Shadow Chancellor and in the language of his leadership of the Labour Party, could be described as a search for a synonym for *mutirao*. His emphasis on 'bonds of mutual trust and consent – absolutely crucial elements of human co-operation' springs from his Christian background. At the close of his seminal essay 'Reclaiming the Ground' he summed up his political perspective thus: 'I do not believe we can truly follow that great commandment [love of our neighbour as ourselves] unless we have a concept of care and concern for our fellow citizens which is reflected in the organisation of our society.'[2]

Connecting care and concern to the organisation of our society was the central task of his political action. For him linking faith and justice was a matter of making laws and budgets. It also led to his decision as leader of the Labour Party to set up the Commission for Social Justice. But his was a politics of clear conviction, of basic foundational moral statements which assumed moral decency at the heart of action as a means of building confidence and trust among people.

Legal to Social Justice

His own life story included a deliberate move from legal justice to social justice. A Queen's Counsel, trained as a lawyer, John Smith moved out of the narrow legal approach to justice limited to the law courts and into active parliamentary politics. It was that move from the observance of the duties of legal justice to a political commitment to the cause of the poor and all victims of injustice that became the hallmark of his practical politics as a Member of Parliament. He believed that to love one's neighbour means to commit oneself to their liberation from injustice, economic and social, nationally and internationally. Tackling poverty was a prime concern throughout his political life. It remains a current challenge.

Recent evidence from the Institute of Fiscal Studies revealing that poverty in Britain trebled between 1979 and 1993 to 11.4 million people (one in five of the population) while the richest 10 per cent became almost twice as well off, suggests that addressing social injustice is as much a political imperative as ever. The widening gap between rich and poor is confirmed by the government's own data. 'Households Below Average Income Statistics' (HMSO, July 1994) spell out that a record one in three children is living in poverty. Overall 13.9 million adults and children (25 per cent of the population) were living below average income in 1991/2, compared with 5 million in 1979. Moreover, the poorest 10 per cent of the population suffered a 17 per cent fall in real income in the same period, while the richest 10 per cent enjoyed an increase of 62 per cent. Only the top three-tenths of the population, ranked by income, achieved above-average income growths between 1979 and 1992. In cash terms there were 1.1 million people earning more than £700 a week in 1991–2 compared with 80,000 in 1979, while the average income of the poorest 10 per cent was down from £74 to £61 a week.

In other words, wealth has clearly not trickled down in our society. Poverty keeps rising, pulling under more and more people as Britain increasingly divides into richer and poorer. While poverty has grown among those out of work, especially among the long-term unemployed, there has been a staggering increase of poverty among those in work, as a low-wage economy became part of that structural shift from traditional manufacturing to service sector, part-time and temporary work, principally for women. Lowering of wage rates has been coupled with the removal of wages councils by the government, and increasing economic insecurity threatens all sectors as temporary contracts become the norm. As fewer and fewer have secure, relatively permanent, full-time work, the future of a housing market based on twenty-five year-mortgages is eroding. Free market foundations look increasingly shaky and the tremors are felt by many more than the existing poor in Britain.

World Poverty

On the world scale, twenty-six countries with just under 15 per cent of the world's population enjoy a mean GNP per capita of over $18,000. This is five times the mean GNP of the world and fifty-five times the GNP of the 3,000 million people (more than half of humanity) who live on a GNP of less than $330. While the purchasing power of Mexicans, for example, has declined by 50 per cent in the last decade, even Malaysians, in a country with rocketing productivity and output tables, find that their take-home pay as industrial workers is actually declining. Under the 'new world order' of free markets and global finance, there is no doubt that the neo-liberal economic virus is still lively in the international system, manifested as World Bank structural adjustment programmes with their menu of free markets, privatisation, a reduced state role, and limited public expenditure. There are, of course, winners and losers in this system of competition; you may lose your job, your income, your home or even your life. For a generation after the Second World War, Western governments using Keynesian economic policies generated a period of staggering growth, but this was checked by growing inflation and rising unemployment, the pressure of public finances and the devastating oil price rise of the mid 1970s. For the Third World, the 1970s were to be the 'Decade of Development'. The rise in the price of oil shifted the Third World into the 'Debt Decade' of the 1980s.

As the Western economies now restructure into temporary, part-time service sector work in the face of high unemployment, the African continent is being practically written out of the text of the global economy, Central- and Latin-American countries and the former Eastern Bloc countries are insistently exhorted to pursue free market economics. The result is increasing and deepening poverty internationally and an unprecedented global disequilibrium. As the dramatic surge of migrants from poor to richer areas is resisted the stage is set for north–south confrontations yet to come.

The Peruvian Gustavo Guttierez has described the origins of liberation theology as 'an ethical indignation at this poverty and marginalization of the great masses of our continent'[3] adding elsewhere 'when I discovered that poverty was something to be fought against, that poverty was structural, that poor people were a class and could organise, it became crystal clear that in order to save the poor one had to move into political action'.[4] There is an echo of this in John Smith's essay 'Reclaiming the Ground'; 'It is a sense of revulsion at injustice and denied opportunity, whether at home or abroad, which impels people to work for a better world, to become . . . democratic socialists.' He

48

adds, 'I believe we must also argue for our cause on the basis of its moral foundation.'[5]

John Smith notably made his maiden speech as the MP for Lanarkshire North on the new Conservative government's Family Income Supplements Bill which dealt with the amounts of social security top-ups to be paid to those in low-paid work. Significantly, in the late 1960s, as John Smith was well aware, there had been a public rediscovery of the reality of poverty in Britain. Praising his predecessor, Margaret Herbison (a former Labour Minister of Social Security) for her efforts in extending welfare services, he fiercely attacked the Tories' Bill for short-changing the working poor. Nor did he shrink from spelling out that a real redistribution of wealth from the poor to the rich was actually being proposed by the Tories. He was not convinced that the Tories were genuine in their desire to help the poor; they were not really interested in 'a lasting attempt to solve the problem of poverty'.[6] The question of tackling what he described as 'the gigantic problem of poverty' remained with him all through his political life.

There is here a clear political lineage with the Christian Socialist tradition. At the turn of the century, R. H. Tawney 'was provoked by the Master of Balliol's question as to why there was so much poverty amidst so much wealth, and then devoted the rest of his long life to pursuing the answer'.[7] John Smith explicitly looked to Tawney who 'founded his political outlook on the moral principles of his Christian commitment', adding 'this sought to enhance individual freedom in a framework of collective common purpose and opportunity in which fellowship was the bond of a community of equality'.[8]

Tawney was within a biblical tradition which regarded the Scriptures as an encounter with the God of liberation,

49

standing against oppression of the poor by the market economy. The word 'justice' occurs 115 times in the Old Testament, implying a way of acting in harmony with the whole community which particularly means defending the poor, the orphan and the widow. The Exodus and the Covenant both reveal Yahweh as liberator, concerned with the defence of the poor. In the New Testament, the message of Jesus 'confers a new and definitive depth on the Old Testament requirement that love of one's neighbour is fulfilled in the observance of justice' as Juan Alfaro puts it.[9] In brief, love of God and love of one's neighbour are fused. The Sermon on the Mount (echoing Isaiah) stresses the role of the poor and oppressed as central, as they in God's theology of justice will be liberated first into the coming Kingdom. According to St Paul, the whole of Christian life is summed up in faith effecting that love and service of neighbour which involves the fulfilment of the demands of justice; 'love of neighbour implies giving to every person what is his or her due with a view to the common good of the whole society' as Juan Alfaro explains.[10]

A Theology of Justice

The attempt to develop a 'theology of justice' relating to the poor and the 'common good' has exercised the Church for centuries from the early Church Fathers to the present. In *Back to Basics: Revisiting Catholic Social Teaching*, Ian Linden points out that 'the poor who suffer disproportionately from injustice frequently have a far greater awareness and understanding of social justice than the rich . . . understanding food as a means of life that should be fairly priced, and "common goods" rather than commodity in a free market.' He refers to a 'life theology' and 'moral economy that survived centuries in the collective consciousness of the poor'.[11]

The concept of the common good as a radical, just redistribution of wealth runs through the sermons of the fourth-century Fathers and is based on the practice of the early Christian community of Acts, Chapter 6. St Ambrose stressed 'you are not making a gift of your possessions to the poor person. You are handing over to him what is his. For what has been given for the common use of all you have arrogated to yourself. The world is given to all and not just to the rich.'[12] St Basil insists 'the bread in your larder belongs to the hungry . . . the money in your vaults belongs to the destitute.'[13] Common good for the early Fathers implied a radical sharing of goods; justice meant fair shares as of right.

In the thirteen century, the Dominican Thomas Aquinas returned to Aristotle in his definition of justice as 'the firm and constant will to give to each one his right',[14] emphasising that to act justly is to accord to others what is theirs by right, by virtue of their humanity. Again following Aristotle, he drew a distinction between that radical sharing justice ('distributive' of things that are essentially common) and a justice of fair dealing ('commutative' relating to the 'just price' and the 'just wage'). At the core of Aquinas' concept of justice is 'the common good'.

Modern Social Teaching

'The common good' is a central strand in Catholic social teaching and it depends on the development of 'social justice', a term first used in 1931 by Pope Pius XI who explained that, in contrast with legal justice, 'the function of social justice is to require of the individual whatever may be required for the common good.' This is a wider reference than distributive justice applied to particular existing goods that should be shared. As Dennis Chiles puts it in *Christianity and Politics*, 'This means that we all have a duty to help create and maintain conditions in society in which people can grow and realise their full potential . . . thus social justice turns us outwards towards others to give practical expression to the commitment to love others as we love ourselves'.[15] Pope John XXIII defined the common good as 'all those social conditions which favour the full development of the human personality' and in the Second Vatican Council document *Gaudium et Spes* the common good is 'the sum of those conditions which allow individuals and groups to achieve their proper purpose more fully and quickly'.[16]

This certainly cannot mean waiting for some sort of 'trickle down' theory to work through to the poor. But then the libertarian 'New Right' have always denied that there is any such thing as social justice, claiming that justice is a concept to be kept within the confines of the law courts. For free market theorists like F.A. Hayek, the processes of allocating wealth and property are part of the mathematical workings of the market and are therefore outside the moral order and 'can be neither just nor unjust'. While the commission on Social Justice in their report *The Justice Gap* point out that market competition cannot be fair and free on 'unlevel playing fields', John Smith goes in deeper in *Reclaiming the Ground* to undermine the individualism of the neo-classical economists and their assumption that human beings conduct their lives on the basis of self-interest and in isolation from others. Even citing Adam Smith he insists 'This thesis grotesquely ignores the intrinsically social nature of human beings and fails to recognise the capability that all people have to act in response to commitments and beliefs that clearly transcend any narrow calculation of personal advantage.'[17] His faith in human potential is characteristic. An insistence on human beings as 'social animals' reaches back to a strand of theology picked up by Thomas Aquinas from the philosopher Aristotle.

Furthermore, his positive understanding of 'social justice' as a dynamic means of promoting the common good in terms not just of redistributing wealth but also status and power in the release of human potential introduces a new vision. The Christian Socialist assault on the economics of the free market had its antecedents in John Ludlow, Charles Kingsley and others. F. D. Maurice was most explicit: 'Competition is put forth as the law of the universe. That is a lie. The time has come for us to declare that it is a lie by word and deed.'[18] What John Smith does is supplement this negative critique of the unjust treatment of the poor and the waste of the free market model with a positive challenge to rebuild a new community and to include all in that task. Rebuilding in the land 'laid waste' a 'new Jerusalem' was precisely the task that faced the biblical community exiled in Babylon.

Healing a Divided Society

In a speech to the Royal Institute of Public Administration in May 1991, John Smith affirmed 'a society which gives priority to welfare will not only be more just but also more cohesive and therefore more socially and politically stable.'[19] Here is his new vision of our society. His leadership election address 'New Paths to Victory' focused on this vision for healing a dividing society. His top priority entitled 'Economic strength and Social Justice' spells it out:

In a modern civilised nation, economic efficiency and

social justice are inseparably linked and mutually supportive. The scourge of poverty, unemployment and low
skills are barriers not only to opportunities for people but
to the creation of a dynamic and prosperous society. It
is simply unacceptable to continue to waste our most
precious resource – the extraordinary skills and talents
of ordinary people.'[20]

He understood the need to build an inclusive society, to
bring in the poor from the margins. The development of that
potent concept of social justice links together that experience
of waste that characterises the democratic critique of free
market economics with a sense of human potential and
promise. As it is put in *The Justice Gap*: 'There is a stronger
sense today that the aims of social justice are served not
only by redistribution; by bringing resources after the event
to people who have done badly – social justice requires as
well that structures should be adapted and influenced in
ways that can give more people a better chance in the
first place.'[21] Social justice, in other words is the route to
a new society, opening up the possibilities of alternatives
(in marked contrast to Mrs Thatcher's blasphemous claim
that 'there is no alternative'). Nor is it the 'end of history'
as economic, social and political possibilities are opened up.
Internationally the liberation theologians speak of 'artisans
of a new humanity' working locally and globally at the
same time.

John Smith was a Christian Socialist with deep moral convictions rooted in his faith in human beings. He emphasised 'I
believe most members of the Labour Party joined for reasons
similar to my own. I saw the Labour Party then and see it now
as a movement to deliver social justice . . . Labour must be
the Party of social justice.' The term 'social justice' recurs

more frequently than any other in his leadership election address. Speaking up for the poor remains central:

> I remain convinced that the Labour Party must be the Party that speaks for the people who are denied a voice in the establishment of our society and that campaigns for justice for the people who are excluded from its prosperity. If Labour were ever to turn its back on families in poverty because their image was too uncomfortable or because their need was too expensive then we would have lost sight of one of the most important contributions Labour can make to British politics.[22]

This is far from a narrow-based politics. It is an invitation to reach out. 'If we are to win next time we must make common cause with the new movements that share our concern for social justice.' Deepening the understanding of our moral foundations also means widening our appeal and reach. In witnessing to social justice in his life and political work John Smith set us on track.

Bibliographical Notes

1 John Smith, *Reclaiming the Ground* (Spire, 1993) p. 134.
2 *ibid*. p. 141.
3 Cited in Leonardo Boff, *The Liberation Theology Debate* (SCM, 1987) p. 4.
4 Cited in S. Torres and J. Eagleson (eds), *Theology in the Americas* (1976) p. 278.
5 *Reclaiming the Ground, op. cit.* p. 137.
6 *Hansard*, 10 Nov. 1970.
7 John Alderton (ed), *Social Christianity* (SPCK, London, 1994) p. 113.
8 *Reclaiming the Ground, op. cit.* p. 127.

JOHN SMITH: AN APPRECIATION

9 Juan Alfaro, *Theology of Justice in the World*, Pontifical Commission of Justice and Peace.
10 *Ibid*.
11 Ian Linden, *Back to Basics: Revisiting Catholic Social Teaching* (CIIR, 1994) p. 22.
12 Thomas Cullinan, *Mine & Theirs: Ours & Theirs* (CTS, 1979).
13 *Ibid*.
14 Thomas Aquinas, *Summa Theologica*, II II q.58 a.1.
15 Dennis Chiles, *Christianity and Politics* (CTS, 1989) p. 33.
16 *Gaudium et Spes*
17 *Reclaiming the Ground*, *op. cit.* p. 132.
18 *The Life of F. D. Maurice*, Vol. 2, p. 32.
19 John Smith's speech to the Royal Institute of Public Administration, May 1991.
20 'New Paths to Victory', John Smith's leadership election address.
21 The Commission on Social Justice, *The Justice Gap* (IPPR, 1994).
22 New Paths to Victory, *op cit.*

6

Christian Socialism and the Good Society

The Revd Dr Leslie Griffiths was born and educated in Wales. After preparing for the Methodist ministry at Cambridge, and taking a PhD in History at London University, he went to work in Haiti, where he became closely associated with the campaign for justice and democracy. Since 1980 he has worked in London and is President of the Methodist Conference for 1994/5. He is a Vice-President of the Christian Socialist Movement.

John Smith was widely recognized as a good man. Not only did people from very different backgrounds say so, but it was clear they meant it. His death got the whole nation thinking. First of all about the shortness of life and the need to make the most of it. Secondly about goodness itself. The word 'good' (like the word 'love') can be over-used to the point of utter blandness. John Smith's death rescued the word from such a fate. For days on end (what seemed, in journalistic terms, an age) the newspapers were filled with thoughts about goodness. And, as the analysis of John Smith's character and legacy went on, so attributes like integrity, honesty, generosity, love of life, came to the surface. So too did the source of these attributes, his Christian faith. And he deserves to be remembered for having kept a vibrant Christian faith together with a wholehearted commitment to the world of politics. He never pushed Christian dogma in an overt manner. But his stance on the major issues of the day cannot be understood without remembering that he was a faithful Christian. He believed in ethical socialism and wasn't afraid to think of it as Christian Socialism. He knew exactly how to relate the world of politics and religion. He was a member of the Christian Socialist Movement and encouraged the Movement to play a full and active part in the discussion of Labour Party policy.

Christian Socialism Comes of Age

The Christian Socialist Movement came of age when it applied for affiliation with the Labour Party. By doing so, it ceased to be a mere talking shop over endless cups of tea. Instead, it committed its members to working out their ideals within the dialectic of everyday political activity. At one fell swoop this imposed a discipline and a realism on Christians who wanted their thinking to shape the kind of society we all live in. And it made a clear statement (however regrettable it should be that this continues to be necessary) about the relationship between religion and politics. They belong inextricably together; Christians pray every day for God's kingdom to come on earth as it is in heaven.

Yet when Christian leaders dare to comment on what's happening in the world of politics, or to criticise proposals being put forward by politicians, they tend to be rebutted as nincompoops, usually on the grounds that they live in some kind of fairyland which bears little or no relationship to the real world in which ordinary people live. They are told to stick to spiritual matters, that is all they're qualified to deal with. This is a fatuous line of argument which I felt needed to be countered strongly when I made my inaugural speech as President of the Methodist Conference early in 1994. This is what I said then:

> What could be more spiritual than the way measures and laws passed in Parliament affect the lives of ordinary people, defining their horizons, shaping their future, raising or crushing their hopes? No government . . . can be allowed to hurt people or drive them to the margins of society. When that happens it's the duty of the Church, the spiritual duty of the Church, to stand by those who suffer.

It seems clear to me that the Christian Socialist Movement's formal relationship with the Labour Party commits Christians to engage in the political process with others of goodwill. It recognises that the Kingdom of God is not a mystical entity dreamed up in pulpits, but rather an ideal to be worked for in the communities where people live and move and have their being.

Religion and Society

Obviously there is no one Christian view on this matter. R. H. Tawney, in the opening chapter of his seminal work *Religion and the Rise of Capitalism*,[1] identified four main religious responses to the world of social institutions and political life. Many religious people, he argued, choose to 'stand on one side in ascetic aloofness'. Monastic communities offer one obvious example of this way of responding. But so too do those brands of evangelical Christianity, underpinned by a dualistic world-view, which shun 'the world' in favour of a counter-culture of their own creating. And indeed, the substance of the criticisms of politicians who denounce Church leaders for daring to put forward an opinion on some political or social issue, suggests that the image *they* have of the Christian Church is of a realm of privatised (and ghetto-ised) faith whose adherents live a long way away from the real world.

Tawney's second category of religious response identifies those who take social and political matters for granted, ignoring them, 'as matters of indifference belonging to a world with which religion has no concern'. The perusal of many church newsletters and magazines, and a careful listening to the subjects of intercessory prayer, reveal larger than expected numbers of churches that fall under this head. The civil and social life of the world and the communities we live in seems to impinge only marginally on the worship and devotion of some Christians.

The third response sees Christians more clearly engaged in social activity, but by way of 'an agitation for some particular reform, for the removal of some crying scandal . . . which will inaugurate the reign of righteousness on earth'. There is a long catalogue of issues which come in here. Slavery, prison reform, child labour, temperance, legislation relating to contagious diseases or church rates, have all been subjects of keen campaigning by the Churches over the last couple of centuries. It has been argued that social action of this kind has managed to unite Churches where doctrine has often divided them. But Pauline Webb[2] suggests that this is by no means always the case. And she cites the World Council of Churches' Programme to Combat Racism and pressure on Churches for 'ethical investment', as issues that have caused deep rifts amongst Christians in all the Churches. But there is no doubt that consensus *has* often been built around single issues. In recent times, Christians have joined others in the Anti-Apartheid Movement, the Campaign for Nuclear Disarmament, the raising of awareness about child prostitution and other similar causes.

But Tawney goes on to distinguish a fourth category of religious response to political and social themes. He describes this as coming from those who

> at once accept and criticize, tolerate and amend, welcome the gross world of human appetites, as the squalid scaffolding from amid which the life of the spirit must rise, and insist that this is also the material of the Kingdom of God. To such a temper, all activities divorced from religion are brutal or dead, but none are too mean to be beneath or too great to be above it, since all, in their different degrees are touched with the spirit which permeates the whole.

Here Tawney is suggesting a readiness on the part of some religious people to take the world as it is, to hold an unblinkered view of the arena of politics and social action, and to get stuck in to the task of reforming and improving it. Their motivation is derived from the understanding that God made the whole world (not just the Church) and that every human being and all groups of men and women are made in his image, his sons and daughters, sisters and brothers to each other and destined, therefore, to live together in community. It follows from this understanding of the way things are that Christians cannot retreat from the world, be indifferent to it, or simply limit their involvement to single issues. People who hold this view share John Wesley's view that the parish can never become their whole world; rather, it's the world that is their parish.

Active Involvement

The affiliation of CSM to the Labour Party shows a clear commitment on the part of its members to contribute to political debate and the political process very much in the sense of Tawney's final category of religious responses. But it does more than that. It not only commits Christians to an active involvement in politics, it also engages them in politics from a socialist point of view. The belief that it is the human lot to live in community is bedrock for all their examination of policy options or social strategies. Views may (and do) differ on many questions. But the greatest good of the largest number, and the dignity and participation in community life by all (even the weakest) members of society, are the ineradicable assumptions upon which all our discourse is built.

At this point, without devoting too much space to the matter, I want to demolish the suspicions of those who think the hidden agenda of Christian Socialists is to form a separate political party. God forbid! The CSM understands full well that we are living in a secular and pluralist society. Equally, it's clear that the Labour Party reflects this reality in its composition and the way it works. There can be no role for the CSM as a fifth column working to turn the Party into a sort of prayer meeting or our society into a theocratic state. There are no such Machiavellian or Byzantine conspiracies abroad, I'm delighted to say.

Many Christians see the CSM as offering them a chance to come out of the closet. They're fed up with the privatisation of faith, a view which reduces religion to the realm of personal piety. They see well enough (they're not fools) that religion is often a component part of many of the world's problems. And they recognise too that religion has often well deserved the dismissive contempt of Karl Marx and others. It *has* been an opiate for the people, it *is* used to serve vested interests, it *does* turn into brute (and brutalising) ideology in the hands of despots and dictators. But none of that quite destroys the grand vision of faith: of a world where justice rolls down like a river to the sea, where the lion lies down with the lamb, where nation shall no longer make war against nation, where love of God is yoked inseparably with love of neighbour, where people are to pray for their enemies as well as their friends. In this two hundredth anniversary year of William Blake's *Songs of Innocence and Experience*, it's good to remember the four cardinal qualities held up by this non-conformist prophet: Mercy, Pity, Peace, and Love – four pillars of a truly Christian social order.

Faith and Compromise

Christian Socialists derive their passion for building this new order from the deepest and the grandest insights of their faith. They treasure that faith along with all the opportunities they have to worship the God who inspires them with its themes. They rejoice particularly at the way God's hope for the world is focused so magnificently and magnanimously in the life, teaching, death and resurrection of Christ. All that is precious to them and foundational to their thinking. Yet when they direct their energies towards the social and political sphere, they happily do this with others of good will whether or not they are motivated in the same way.

63

They know that this will sometimes involve compromise, and that they will occasionally be working alongside people who despise some of the things they cherish. But, because they have a clear-headed view of the nature of political activity, they'll not shrink from the task. In this approach, they've learned a great deal from the thinking of Reinhold Niebuhr.

Niebuhr, especially in his recently reissued *Moral Man and Immoral Society*, shows how wrong it is to take the moral ideals that matter to people as individuals and presume that they can simply be translated and applied to society as a whole as if society were simply the individual writ large. Society is, in fact a whole lot of individuals, a bewildering variety of interest groups. The interplay and the exchange of ideas between them in the attempt to forge some kind of consensus is what constitutes the core of political activity. No single group, and certainly no powerful individual, can simply write the script for whatever emerges from political debate. Writing of people's yearning for peace and justice, Niebuhr argues thus:

It is a vision prompted by the conscience and insight of individual man, but incapable of fulfilment by collective man. It is like all true religious visions, possible of approximation but not of realisation in actual history. [At the collective level, man] . . . must content himself with a more modest goal. His concern for some centuries to come is not the creation of an ideal society in which there will be uncoerced and perfect peace and justice, but a society in which there will be enough justice, and in which coercion will be sufficiently non-violent to prevent his common enterprise from issuing into complete disaster. That goal will seem too modest for the romanticists;

but the romanticists have so little understanding of the perils in which modern society lives, and overestimate the moral resources at the disposal of the collective human enterprise so easily, that any goal regarded as worthy of achievement by them must necessarily be beyond attainment.

For 'romanticists' in the above paragraph, it is perfectly possible to substitute 'Christians' in some of the ways they have traditionally responded to the world of political and social activity. Niebuhr was writing in the period between the wars when, as hindsight now shows us only too well, 'moral man' was so notably absent from the world in which 'immoral society' was choosing options that brought hell and destruction to so many. Christians can never allow themselves to be romantics in that way again. Whatever the risks of compromise and dirty hands, those risks have to be taken. Political activity is as necessary an aspect of living in God's world as any other.

A Christian Socialist Programme

What I've chosen to do in this essay is to take a look at the political process and the need for Christians to be involved in it rather than outline programmes that might ensue from that involvement. It's only possible here to sketch the main features of the programme that Christian Socialists would need to work for. It would include the following elements:

Wealth creation Socialists are often accused of having myriad plans for spending and distributing wealth and few for creating it. It is important to show how we would regenerate British manufacturing industry, stimulate productivity, motivate a trained workforce, attract investment, and guarantee good working practice. This would be done with due consideration for proper protection and rights of association for people in work, a recognition of the rights of investors to expect appropriate profit from their investment, a respect for the environment, and a just taxation policy.

Social justice   In the last few years it has become harder and harder to gain access to services that ought to be considered rights. In a just society everyone, rich and poor, strong and weak, should have equal access to health care, education and training, job opportunities, legal advice, and housing. The slide towards a 'two-nation' state has left far too many people floundering and marginalised.

Internationalism   Britain belongs to a continent and a world where interdependence is a fact of life. We must work commitedly for an increasingly united Europe while strengthening our links with the Commonwealth. We must play our part in a much-needed revitalisation of the United Nations Organisation. We must look again at our trading practices with the Third World. Our aid programme must honour the target of 0.7 per cent of gross national product which we've paid lip service to for a long time but have seen slipping away from our grasp over the years. We must also look again at Third World indebtedness, remembering the biblical principle of jubilee. A world in which the strong honour the weak is a world where we can live with our consciences and minimise the chances of war.

Constitutional reform   Much work will have to be done to restore and enhance the proper balance between local and national government. Far too much is controlled currently from Whitehall. Much of the control of our public life will also have to be de-quangoed. But, above all, the work of the Plant Committee on Electoral Reform will need to be taken seriously and some kind of proportional representation considered urgently. Too many people feel disenfranchised and alienated from the political process by the current system.

Sustainability Political discourse, specially during election campaigns, makes large promises about the ability of one party or another to boost growth and improve voters' standard of living. Before too long this will be clearly seen to be empty rhetoric. In any case, quality of life is far more important than standards of living. An educational programme is needed to help the population at large identify as a political priority the building of communities, a priority which moves preoccupations away from disposable income to achievable social objectives. It may be necessary for people to have less money in their pockets if such hopes are to be realised.

Bernard Meadows' sculpture at the entrance to Congress House in Great Russell Street depicts a strong man bending down to help a weak man to his feet. It's entitled *The Spirit of Trade Unionism* but, in reality, offers a metaphor of much wider usefulness. It is not usual for strong men to use their strength in this way. In the realm of organised labour just as much as in other sectors of our national life, we've seen too many instances of strong men using their strength to tyrannise others. Meadows' sculpture challenges that stereotype. The Christian Socialist Movement seeks to work for just such a vision: a nation and a world where people understand their interdependence and their need for each other, a world where the strong rejoice in their strength and the weak are honoured and participating members of society.

John Smith: An Appreciation

Bibliographical Notes

1   R. H. Tawney, *Religion and the Rise of Capitalism* (Pelican, London, reprinted 1948).
2   P. Webb in *Agenda for Prophets* (London, 1980).
3   R. Niebuhr, *Moral Man and Immoral Sciety* (SCM, London, 1963).

7

Putting Power into People's Lives

Michael Meacher was first elected as MP for Oldham West in 1970. He served as Undersecretary of State for Industry, Health and Social Security and Trade in the Labour Government of 1974–9, and was on Labour's National Executive Committee from 1983 to 1988. Since the last general election he has been Labour's spokesperson on Development and Co-operation, and is presently Opposition spokesperson on the Citizen's Charter.

Market capitalism is anything but the impersonal and objective system dedicated to efficiency that so many Western economists claim. It is in reality a strongly value-loaded system riddled with predispositions that heavily colour the outcomes. It is above all a power system.

Free markets favour the strong and penalise the weak. Whilst theoretically they contain an in-built mechanism for self-correction of excessive economic disequilibrium, in power terms it is the reverse. Acquiring personal or corporate economic power serves only to accelerate the acquisition of more, while those possessing little or no power in the market often find even that reduced.

The great institutions of state – big business, City finance, the media, the Civil Service and the government machine, the legal system and major public services – all reach an accommodation with the market and are infected with its ethos. All are power systems within their own right, and given the extreme inequality of the market environment within which they co-exist, their power is heavily concentrated at the top. Together they form the dominant power bloc that controls Britain today.

Radical Options

How are radicals to deal with this concentration of power which ensconces privilege and opportunity in the hands of right-wing elites? The post-war answer was to wrest the 'commanding heights' of the economy from their grasp and vest them instead under public control. The results, while full of promise in the 1940s, lost their appeal over the next thirty years.

Monopoly industries and large-size firms, while conferring technical economies of scale, were plagued by over-centralised decision-making and remoteness which lowered labour morale. Ministers held to the Morrisonian concept of the independent public board, so the objective of planning in the public interest proved difficult to achieve. At the same time Whitehall interference, especially Tory Ministers holding down prices, undermined efficiency and generated deficits and further loss of morale. And as mass-production capitalism gave way to flexible specialisation, nationalised industries came to be seen in many Western countries like stranded whales beached after their heyday in the era from the 1930s to the 1970s.

Nor did nationalised industries succeed much better in their social objectives, partly due to the timidity of Labour governments. Ministers continued to pick directors and top managers from the private sector who were steeped in the ethic far more of capitalist markets than of socialist community – hence the quip that 'nationalisation plus Lord Robens doesn't equal socialism'. The consumer interest was never effectively represented. And the goal of public service, or the idea of community benefit as opposed to market profitability, was never translated into practical policy. A social interest criterion of viability was never developed to override pure commercial market principles.

Choice and the Market

But if public ownership, at least in the traditional form associated with statism and monolithic bureaucracy, doesn't give that access to power that socialists earlier hoped, neither did the Thatcherite model of the market. Giving 'Sid' £200-worth of privatised British Gas shares may be a wonderful something-for-nothing bribe, but it doesn't increase consumer rights over pricing, bill queries, cut-offs or quality of service. Choice in the capitalist market is about being the passive recipient of this or that material thing. It isn't about empowering people to live their own lives in the fullest sense in their own way.

Right-wing market formulae do not give access to, let alone control over, any of the big decisions that fundamentally determine the quality of people's lives. Decisions about what goods are produced and what services offered, who is hired or fired, and how much is invested for future work and where and in what form, are all taken by employers and holders of big capital. Do consumers feel the market offers them power to shape to their liking services like road and rail transport, the mass media, local repairs and maintenance or adult education? In the all-important area of enforcing rights in a free society, the market offers only extremely unequal access to the law. Nor does it offer any effective means to counter abuse of power by the police, newspaper owners, local authority planners, the health authorities and doctors or companies and their managers.

So neither a remote, bureaucratic, centralised state nor an unfettered Thatcherite market system can release the power and opportunities for individuals to gain real control over their environment so as to develop their full potential as they choose. But there is a third and better way.

A New Role for the State

Instead of the post-war socialist aspiration for the state to *supersede* market forces, which was not only over-ambitious but would raise as many problems of control as it resolved, the state should take the role of catalyst. Instead of seeking to be the universal provider, it should act in different contexts as regulator, advocate, enabler or protector.

For what is vital is linking the state to the cause of socialist individualism. No doubt for some for whom socialism is defined exclusively as state control over the commanding heights of the economy, this expression may seem a contradiction in terms. But that is to ignore that state versus markets is not so much an irreconcilable antithesis as a continuum where different trade-offs are possible. On the one side are the fundamentalist statists who pioneered the inflexible and bureaucratic 1940s nationalisations. On the other are the fundamentalist marketeers who currently champion untrammelled self-interest and endlessly want to roll back the state. In between are the advocates, on the one hand, of a much more flexible state regulation, and on the other of a much more constrained market system. Both project a role for the state that is less heavy-handed, more innovative, more imaginative, and indeed more of a stimulant if not directly entrepreneurial.

Beyond Regulation

It means going a great deal beyond mere regulation in its present form. It means intervening not just to correct weaknesses in the operation of the market or to deal with externalities, but shifting production in ways that widen the spread of opportunities and power. The state could play a major role, for example, in developing and monitoring employee democracy within companies and in extending arbitration for the resolution of internal disputes (not least to pre-empt strikes). It could promote environmentalist goals by a mix of direct controls, tax incentives and subsidies. It could take the lead, through an independent panel of specialist consultants, in auditing management quality in both the public and private sectors.

As enabler the state could ensure that high-quality opportunity training is available for any who wish to switch careers in mid or later life into wholly new employment fields. It could award to disabled persons, young or elderly, grants according to their assessed degree of disability so that they could buy in the services that they themselves chose. It could provide, through a co-operative development agency, technical, financial and managerial support for any group of employees who want to work under self-management auspices. Its financial support for physically, mentally or socially handicapped persons or for lone-parent families should act not as an obstacle course precluding employment, but as a launching-pad to a job, a pathway out of poverty.

Nor should the state shrink from entrepreneurial initiatives, particularly where its special role makes it the most appropriate agent to perform a function. It could provide free legal aid and advice in inner-city areas, where now the law has become inaccessible to all but the richest and poorest of citizens. It could offer a one-stop-shop point in each local area for the comprehensive collection of house exchange data, as the best route to cheap and efficient conveyancing. It could provide both initial training and follow-through employment for a quality corps of contractors specialising in the whole range of household services.

Giving People Power

The facilitator role for the state is a key part of what should be the central theme of modern socialism. That theme is focused on the issue of power. Capitalist power lies in the concentration of control in a few hands of the main organisations that determine the future development of society. The essential characteristic of socialism by contrast is that control over people's lives is placed increasingly in their own hands.

Such a theme is consistent with the traditional formulations of socialism. These have centred round such ideas as the common ownership of the means of production, workers' control, welfare and equality, altruism and co-operative industrial relations, appropriating property incomes, and the brotherhood of human beings. These are all valid ideas in their own right, and there can be no question of reducing them to a single concept. Yet redistribution of power is at the heart of them all.

It is what common ownership, workers' control and the appropriation of property incomes were precisely designed to achieve. As regards welfare and equality (the Croslandite formula), it doesn't involve giving people things, whether money or services, which can entrench dependency, but it does mean finding ways to enable people to overcome dependency or other limitations themselves, by their own means. Regarding co-operative industrial and social relations and the ideal of human brotherhood, it is certainly true that giving people greater control over their own lives is no guarantee of altruism. But it is precisely the essence of both socialism and Christianity that opportunities must be balanced by enlarging responsibilities and obligations to others too.

Giving people power to gain control over their own lives has a myriad of applications. It offers a connecting thread which would direct reform into every corner of public life with the same thorough-going and comprehensive questioning, the same relentless drive, and the same highly charged political excitement and conviction as imbued some of the Thatcher years.

Yet it shouldn't be the sole theme, or even the main theme, of the radical Left. Empowerment within the market is one thing, but people are far, far greater than the market or any other economic system that may be devised. It is the economy that should serve people, not people the economy.

The real argument against privatised market capitalism is that it reduces people to a flat, single-dimension, dehumanised existence.

Our Political Philosophy

People are not in any sense primarily economic beings. Their social needs, cultural interests, artistic and aesthetic heritage and spiritual aspirations are each just as important and together are certainly more central to their existence. An undiluted philosophy of *enrichissez-vous* very quickly begs the question of what it is all *for*, and at what price it is bought. None of this is of course to suggest that economic efficiency and competitiveness are not necessary. It is rather that they need to be *integrated* with other goals, and there can be no doubt they were exaggerated out of all proportion in Thatcherite Britain.

No political philosophy can fully satisfy unless it seeks to answer the deepest questions about the purpose and meaning of human existence. No philosophy of the market-place even engages this dimension. The totem of gross national produce (GNP) cannot begin to embrace qualitative goals such as democracy, freedom, human dignity, self-realisation or personal fulfilment. It does not even make qualitative distinctions within the economic sphere so as to identify growth that is pathological, unhealthy, disruptive or destructive. It provides no measure of such crucial indices of the state of national feeling as alienation, frustration, insecurity or congestion.

GNP takes no account of the fact that materialism, which it does measure, is so limiting. It simply denotes the amassing of material wealth for the self which, while providing

76

immediate gratification, ignores the deeper sources of human satisfaction in commitment to others, to the community and to external causes. As Christ said two millennia ago, and it remains no less true today, a man can gain the whole world and lose his own soul, and it profits him nothing. There has never been a truer epitaph of the shallowness of capitalism.

There is no more tyrannical or deadening a judgment than that such-and-such a proposal is 'uneconomic'. An activity may be 'economic' though it plays havoc with the environment or with social needs, yet a competing activity, even if at some cost it protects and conserves the environment or advances personal or social happiness, is ruled out of court as 'uneconomic'. The market is indeed the institutionalisation, not merely of individualism, but of irresponsibility.

The Failure of Scientific Materialism

In the end, by pursuing their own interests to the limit, as capitalism exhorts them to do, people will never find happiness. The essence of human aspirations cannot be reduced to self-gratification. It is rather to *values* and ideals which extend far above and beyond the self.

It is unfashionable to talk of values, especially spiritual values, because this conflicts with the dominant ethic of the twentieth century, scientific materialism, which is striving precisely to be value-less. Yet it is surely the fundamental flaw of our modern value-arid society that this century all the prevalent concepts of people have sought and failed to explain the human condition in terms of some lower order code, as though man's unique comprehending of values did not exist.

Marxism interpreted religion, philosophy, art and culture as disguised economic interests. Darwinian evolution stressed the development of higher forms from lower, and competition via natural selection to bring about the survival of the fittest. Freud reduced human will to the sub-conscious conflicts of the mind. Relativism has been a force to deny all absolutes, norms and standards. Positivism as a movement has renounced all knowledge other than that obtained through the techniques of the natural sciences. And then Hayek, and his disciple Thatcher, subordinated all man's strivings to the economic imperative of the market. What all these have in common, besides their *folie de grandeur* in claiming to explain all human phenomena, is their basic premise that any concept of higher-order being is reducible by a process of semi-mathematical logic to a lower one.

Social Ambitions

Such systematic reductionism not only generates total despair by denying any purpose or meaning to human life on earth, it is also profoundly mistaken. As philosophers from Aristotle onwards have recognised, there is a metaphysical element to human nature, a higher order of being, that separates humans from all other creatures. That unique aspect of human nature can only be fulfilled through a person's social ambitions of the highest order. He or she can only be at one with themselves at the deepest level if they are at one with those around them – neighbours, local community, fellow-citizens within their nation, and indeed at the international level, in terms of the kind of world in which they live.

This is what has always inspired socialists to put their faith in the realisation of human brotherhood, in the impulse of altruism and sharing, and in the ideal of freedom for all through equal chances for all. It is what has always impelled the socialist conscience to cry out against poverty, the ugliness of deprivation, and the crime of stifled liberties and opportunities.

While therefore empowering people within the economy and society should be a key part of the socialist credo, it is not by itself sufficient. *The use to which that power is put* is just as important. If it is used exclusively for self-aggrandisement or self-gratification, it is not a socialist empowerment. It is only socialist if that enhanced power is used creatively to benefit others or to contribute to a better community or to building the welfare of others beyond the self. By a paradox unique to human nature, only then is it genuinely satisfying to the individual concerned.

8

Customers and Citizens

Trained as a barrister, Jack Straw made his name in politics as both an Islington councillor and a member of the Inner London Education Authority. He also worked as Barbara Castle's political adviser. He was first elected as MP for Blackburn in 1979. From 1987 to 1992 he was Labour's chief spokesperson on Education, and since 1992 has been the Shadow Secretary of State for the Environment, covering Local Government.

The war was an abominable waste, a terrible price, but if we had not rescued Belgium and France we would have lost more than a generation – we would have lost freedom, respect for the truth, and for treaties, all the abstract things that are more important than material ones.

Mr Donald Hodge, a 99-year-old veteran of the First World War, Armistice Day, Ypres, 1993, in the *Daily Telegraph*, 12 November 1993.

John Smith was the first to recognise the importance of material things. Much of his anger – and by God, he could be angry – was fuelled by his sense of outrage at the effects which a lack of material things brought many of his constituents, and many others across the world. But he was angry above all about the way in which the Thatcherite Tories had reduced and debased political debate to the level of a crude, meretricious auction, in which greed and selfishness flourished, and concern for others was so often mocked as weakness.

John's especial contribution to British politics was to seek to break out of this new Tory strait-jacket, to elevate political debate. For him, politics was about morality, and values, or it was an ultimately worthless pursuit.

It was not just that John believed that man does not live by bread alone. It was rather that he saw that the material wants and needs of his constituents could not properly and permanently be met without the force of moral persuasion, to convince those who were prosperous and secure that they too would lead better, more contented lives if others less prosperous were sharing better in the wealth of the nation. As he said 'let me assert my profound conviction that politics ought to be a moral activity and we should never feel inhibited in stressing the moral basis of our approach.'[1]

This lay behind his constant reference to the notion of active citizenship. He rejected the idea – much advanced by people like William Waldegrave – that in modern Britain, 'consumer' rights over the public service could be a substitute for democratic rights over these services. He applauded any improvements in the services which public departments could offer; but he was contemptuous of the whole project of the so-called and misnamed 'Citizen's Charter', which has reduced people's role from that of citizen to customer.

It is one of the defining differences between his vision of democratic socialism, and the tawdry two-nation Toryism now being played out by John Major.

The Ethic of Customer Care

All of us, of course, applaud the trend to ensure that those who provide public services are sensitive to the needs of those who receive the services. It is entirely right that those who sit on one side of the counter in the appointments section of a large hospital should know what it feels like to be on the other. All public servants should be known by name. The telephone should be answered quickly, mail dealt with promptly. Courtesy and consideration cost nothing, but can produce immeasurable rewards, for giver and recipient.

We should not therefore deride the 'customer care' approach which has in recent years been adopted by many public and private services alike. Much of this approach was pioneered by Labour local authorities, and in turn formed part of the experience behind the Citizen's Charter.

Our concern should be a different and more fundamental one. It is to take issue with those on the Right – including many in the present government – who are engaged in a pervasive and insidious programme to define almost all our public relationships by the market and the cash nexus. Their aim is not to supplement citizen's rights by consumer rights, but rather to replace those rights of citizenship. The purpose is both cynical and sinister. It is to reduce people's sense of democratic rights, to make them passive consumers of services rather than active citizens.

We are all customers now, or so we are told. Literally, the word means 'a buyer, purchaser, a person entering a shop to buy'. It has a meaning specific to the purchase of goods, or services. The word implies that the person who is the 'customer' has a substantial degree of choice, over which shop to enter and over what he or she may buy. But where once this word was confined to our trading relations, it has now been extended to define the relationship between provider and receiver, in many – and soon, I suggest, all – public services.

Passengers, patients, students, taxpayers, claimants are all customers now.

The commuter waiting for the 7.10 on a windswept platform may have no effective choice over his mode of transport to work, and certainly none over the train operator, but he or she is a 'customer'.

In the NHS, the market culture has taken an iron grip of many managers. The concourses of hospitals now look and feel like shopping malls, or airport termini. You cannot move for leaflets telling you of your 'rights' – as 'NHS customers'. But patients actually have fewer rights than ever as to whether their hospital will be there at all; and if the dramatic increase in complaints is any indication, dissatisfaction with the NHS has never been greater. Those patients in ordinary, non-fund-holding GP practices who need specialist hospital treatment in another health district now have less effective choice over where and when they might be treated than ever before. But they, increasingly, are 'customers'.

In many of our further education colleges, 'customer' services have replaced student services. At least, here it could be argued that the student has some choice of college and of course.

The New 'Customers'

But most absurd of all, taxpayers, and claimants are now officially described as 'customers'.

As taxpayers none of us has any choice over the level of tax which we should pay. A tax system based on such voluntary principles quickly falls into decay – and is, of course, profoundly unfair. While I want to be treated civilly by the Inland Revenue (and I am) my relationship with them is not that of customer and shopkeeper. Nor should it be described as such.

Social security claimants have no effective choice of any kind. Indeed, the eligibility rules for means-tested benefits require that but for the benefit claimed the claimant would lack the money even to live, let alone to shop around. Claimants cannot choose where they make their claim nor when they make it; nor do they have any choice over the amount or duration of benefit.

To call them 'customers' is to distort the meaning of words. Worse, it is to mock the condition of those who are described by the term, to pretend that they have choice where none in truth exists, and to obfuscate the nature of the relationship which exists between claimant and provider.

It will not be long, I promise, before we hear the new Head of the semi-privatised Prison Service, Mr Derek Lewis, announcing that in future his prisoners should be known as 'customers'.

A False Analogy

The objection, therefore, to defining the recipients of public services as 'customers' is that the word is the wrong one. It is an analogy, and a poor one at that. It fails properly to define the relationship between provider and recipient in six important respects.

First, the term implies that the only relationship that matters between the individual and a public service is one based upon use. This is what Marx used to describe as 'commodity fetishism'. But a service such as education is not a simple commodity in the way that an item of furniture is. It is used by very many people with different needs at the same time. What is more, at any one time there will be a great deal more people who have an interest in the quality of a service such as education than use it at any one time. Here the limitations of the customer model are very apparent.

Secondly, the term deceives people about the choice which they may or may not have over a particular public service. 'Customer care' has commendably led, for example, to the waiting area in the Blackburn Benefits Agency Office being improved. The waits are less, the comfort is greater. But what truly matters to citizens is the level of benefits, and the condition of their award. When I was recently in the Benefits Office I asked one unemployed claimant what he thought about the service he had received in the new, and genuinely much improved, waiting area. Are you satisfied, I asked him. 'It depends whether I get my giro, doesn't it?' he replied. Yes, he said, it was better waiting now than it once had been. But, he implied, and he was right, that was wholly subsidiary to whether he got the benefit, or not – and whether he could live on it. 'Customer care' in the DSS could have coincided with improvement in benefits, or at least not their absolute reduction. But the fact is that these 'customer comforts' have increased just as the customers' rights as citizens to decent benefits have been seriously reduced. When I say that for many Ministers the exercise has been a cynical one, I mean it.

Third, the customer principle, with which the Citizen's Charter is suffused, depoliticises society. It suggests that the only way in which individuals can exercise control over the goods and services they need and want is through the cash nexus – the act of buying in the market-place. It was this idea which made John Smith almost apoplectic. For he saw how much it undermined the elective principle that we can exercise choice about the type, nature and availability of services through the ballot box.

There is little place for democratic accountability in the customer model. A customer can choose a commodity but he or she cannot choose the manner of its making or delivery. Yet people should have the right to a say over the way in which their services are delivered, not just to a process which determines who can deliver it cheapest.

The customer agenda in the Health Service has coincided with a deliberate reduction in citizens' political rights over its running. Once, elected representatives sat on health authorities, which met in public. Then they were removed, and power was transferred to unaccountable, self-appointed trusts and boards. Now, some of the quangos – the regional health authorities – are to be abolished, to be replaced by single, unelected appointees and officials. The end result is that the NHS 'consumer' now has more choice over the things which in the end do not matter, like being able to buy a wider range of goods in the shops in the concourse, and much less say over the things which really do matter, like whether there is a hospital there at all, and who is held accountable if things go wrong. These quangos would have had a very short life in a Smith government. He combined an intellectual irritation for them with that contempt (sometimes haughty) which only a self-confident Scots lawyer can truly show for the English establishment, too many of whose hangers-on had gained access to membership of quangos.

Fourth, the customer model of the public service leads to a lower level of administration and to greater inefficiency than would otherwise be the case. The NHS well illustrates this point. The customer model requires the creation of markets. In the NHS, one – or a series – has had to be created artificially. As the US experience shows so well the universal characteristic of all health care systems based on market is that a greater share of GDP is devoured for a given level of service, there is more bureaucracy, and less overall patient choice. Exactly that is now happening with the market-based NHS. The increase in the number of administrators, the decline in the number of nurses, is not an accident, nor an aberration. It is what happens when a public service culture is replaced by a private sector analogy.

Fifth, the customer mode leads to the denigration of the public service and the idea that it can sustain an identity and culture which is distinct from that of the market-based, money-making private sector. The Tories know this. They suspect that public servants are more likely to vote Labour – another reason why their assault on the services has been so relentless.

Sixth, and above all, to pick up the evocative words of the quotation which which I opened, the customer model leads to the worship of material things, and to the belief that social relationships depend upon possession, to the exclusion of 'all the abstract things that are more important than material ones'. 'Customer' is a material concept. 'Citizen' is an abstract one. I know which John Smith thought more important.

The customer care initiatives taken by the Conservatives are often as hollow and cynical as those taken by the shoddiest of private sector companies. It is significant that they concentrate on complaints procedures. People should be able to complain and to get their money back if they're not satisfied. But by definition these rights can only be activated after the event. What the government is far less keen to promote is consultation. That is because giving people a say over the running of services makes them more than customers. It makes them citizens.

The Old Fabian Model

But in criticising the new customer model, we all accept the deficiencies of the old Fabian model for the delivery of public services. It was paternalistic, remote, 'Whitehall knows best'. It denied people sufficient choice, for instance over what type of housing they wanted. It also had a tendency to promote passivity and 'clientilism', particularly in the operation of some aspects of the welfare state. This was a common criticism of the 'state' in the 1970s, held as much on the left as on the right, and reflected in popular culture and stereotypes about council and government bureaucracy.

The New Right critique based in part on the work of philosophers like Robert Nozick grew out of the 1960s-influenced rejection of state bureaucracy. The argument was that the state necessarily infringed individual liberty and frustrated individual initiative and enterprise. The 'night-watchman state' coupled with deregulation and an attempt to recreate the idealised conditions of the market in public services were what followed. This is still Peter Lilley's and Michael Portillo's agenda.

What John Smith wanted was a society which taught, and celebrated, the importance of the abstract as well as of the material. That means seeing any customer agenda as very much supplementary to citizens' rights, not as a substitute for them. It means developing an agenda of active citizenship, which teaches people how to participate and not just to consume. To achieve this there is much reform which needs to take place in Westminster and Whitehall. People's rights need to be transparent, which is why John saw a Bill of Rights as so important. But a great many key decisions affect people's localities. For that, John was committed to a new agenda for local democratic rights.

Tony Blair will pay John Smith the greatest tribute he could by putting into effect so much of John's project, so that people once again will find enrichment in their lives by a government committed to moral, as well as material pursuits.

BIBLIOGRAPHICAL NOTE

1   John Smith, *Reclaiming the Ground* (Spire, London, 1993) p. 128.

9

A Country with a Sense of Community

The Right Honourable Neil Kinnock was born and brought up in Wales and studied at Cardiff University. He was first elected as MP for Bedwellty in 1970, and later for Islwyn from 1983 to 1994. He was elected to Labour's National Executive Committee in 1978, and from 1979 to 1983 was Shadow Secretary of State for Education. From 1983 to 1992 he was Leader of the Labour Party and Leader of the Opposition. In 1994 he was appointed a European Commissioner.

A few years before this century began, Matthew Arnold declared that the inequalities that he witnessed in his country demeaned and weakened all of society. 'On the one side', he said, 'inequality harms by pampering; on the other by vulgarising and depressing. A system founded on it is against nature and, in the long run, breaks down'.[1]

A few years before this century ends, I do not think it is nostalgia that persuades me Arnold was right and that he remains right, and that John Smith would have agreed. A brief, but I think not misleading, summary of the history of the intervening ninety years reinforces the validity of that view. Thirty years after Arnold's declaration, a society 'founded' on' inequality *was* breaking down under the pressures of prolonged mass unemployment, industrial collapse, ignorance, disease and social deprivation.

New Foundations

Mobilisation for total war, and the gigantic economic and social reforms that came out of that conflict did not bring an end to inequality or a universal triumph for equality. But it did mean that society became 'founded on' principles and practices of opportunity, care, employment, shelter, of rights of provision and responsibilities for contribution.

By legislation, executive decision, taxation, investment and distribution the society that had been 'founded on' inequality became 'founded on' community, on interdependence, on mutuality. It was obviously not perfection. Most of us know that all of those changes in common rights to claim and common obligations to subscribe inevitably left much to be done by democracy, much to be desired by its citizens. But I would suggest that, whatever its deficiencies, such a society was not in danger, in Arnold's words, of 'breaking down'.

I do not feel that I am devaluing the progress that has unquestionably been made or being extravagantly pessimistic in taking the view that the same cannot be said for our society now.

To assert that is clearly, however, not enough. Therefore, I want to assess the extent and causes of this condition, to offer a contribution to the discussion about the ways to advance from it and consequently to suggest ways of ensuring that we have a country with a sense of community.

Economic Trends

I believe it is possible to discern two indisputable economic trends over recent years that should profoundly influence our understanding of the need to achieve that objective.

Poverty The first of these trends is the marked growth of poverty.

The latest figures, published in July 1994 by the Government's own statistical department, reveal that the income of the poorest 10 per cent of our population has fallen by 17 per cent in real terms since 1979.

The number living below the European 'poverty line' – half the average income – has risen from 5 million to 13.9 million people. That is a quarter of all the people in the United Kingdom.

The figures also showed that nearly one third of all children in Britain are now living in poverty – an increase from 3.9 million to 4.1 million since 1990/91.

Poverty is patently not a condition exclusively endured by the old, the very young, the sick or the unemployed. The working poor – the number of people in jobs but experiencing poverty – has trebled to 12 per cent since 1979. Of those living in poverty, the proportion of lone parents has risen from 19 to 59 per cent, the numbers of single pensioners has risen from 12 to 40 per cent and the number of two-parent families with children living in poverty has risen from 8 per cent to 24 per cent.

Clearly the statistics do not expose the full realities of despair, powerlessness, fragmentation, alienation and poverty of the spirit which are the infected sores caused by the wounds of poverty.

And the destructive consequences of increased poverty are compounded by a second and parallel trend that has developed over recent years.

Division and Inequality   Disparity has been compounded by division. While larger sections of our population have been dragged into poverty, other groups in the same society have grown more and more detached from them.

The startling growth in the inequality of incomes within the British population has proved to be one of the central features of the 1980s and early 1990s. The gulf in our country between the prosperous and the poor is widening as it has not done before in this century.

As the Institute for Fiscal Studies Report *For Richer for Poorer* put it, 'The increase in income inequality during the 1980s dwarfed the fluctuations in inequality seen in previous decades . . . ' The income share of the poorest tenth of society has fallen back from 4.2% in 1961 to 3.0% in 1991, with most of the fall occurring during the 1980s.

While the poorest 20 per cent are at best no better off than they were, the richest 10 per cent of the British population has become 60 per cent richer since 1979.

And, in that time, the top 1 per cent – with average incomes above £120,000 a year – have gained £75 billion mainly because of cumulative tax cuts which have taken their contributions from 45.2 per cent of income in 1985 down to 36.2 per cent in 1995.

It is a matter of plain record that continued taxation and social security policies have exacerbated the income differences, rather than minimised their effects. Whatever benign intentions may be claimed or genuinely held by those who support those policies, it has to be said that the growth of inequality thus appears to be not an accident or economic fortune but a deliberate product of economic strategy.

Tax policies, however, tell only part of the story. The other main cause has been an increase in wage inequality during the decade in which Wages Councils were abolished and many previously secure public sector jobs were contracted out to employers whose competitiveness in the contest for tenders depended upon real reductions in wages.

The old conviction that rising economic growth for the country and rises in the standard of living for the average family would see a commensurate reduction in poverty has gone. In the recent past a growing section of the population has been excluded from any benefits of growth.

And if, as a nation, we have seen old certainties eroded over these years, it is also the case that many of the changes in economic circumstances that have occurred have had effects that go well beyond those of our fellow citizens formally classified as poor.

Fear of losing jobs in every level of the workforce and the fear of losing accompanying homes and security foster a more general lack of certainty about the future. Such fear is the most inhibiting of all human instincts. In some, the spirit of enterprise and creativity manages to survive. But in many, the reaction is one of caution, of conformity, of social introversion that can, obviously, be exploited by racists and others who deal in the simplistic politics of resentment.

These outcomes may not have been intended. But they were foreseeable. The ruling political orthodoxy of the last decade and a half has been that there has to be some kind of trade-off between inequality and efficiency. The former is seen as unfortunate but necessary collateral damage worth accepting as a means of achieving the latter.

A Costly Vision of Society

But the tangible effects of the policies that have flowed from these notions have starkly revealed the inadequacy of this vision of society and its consequent model of economic development.

Perhaps the clearest evidence of the price that such policies have exacted is the cost of unemployment. It amounts to £28 billion this year – £9,000 for every unemployed person in the country.

That, by any measure is a vast economic waste – a drag on economic prosperity – which, in itself, contributes to national economic disability.

Of course, unemployment does not come alone and it cannot merely be measured as an addition to the Public Sector Borrowing Requirement. Crime, for instance, while never excused by or uniquely caused by prolonged and widespread unemployment, has risen significantly in the years in which joblessness has been high and broadly spread.

Between 1980 and 1993, the number of people who had no experience of crime fell from two-thirds to a half of the adult population. British citizens are now more likely to be victims of burglary than any other nationality in the European Union and while crime in general has more than doubled since 1979, violent crime has risen by 130 per cent, and robberies have risen by over 300 per cent.

Fuelling this rise in crime has been a parallel rise in drug abuse. Since 1982, among the under-seventeens, there has been a fivefold increase in the number of drug offenders and the total number of notified addicts has increased by a similar proportion.

No one needs to be told that the costs of crime have become immense. The public expenditure cost of the criminal justice system has increased by 100 per cent since 1979 to £9 billion this year. Individual householders have seen the cost of insurance for household contents rise by 50 per cent since 1979.

In such circumstances – of rising crime, drug abuse and a

general sense of loss of security – it should not be surprising that observers and commentators turn to the family, trying to find an explanation for the ills of society.

Understanding Families   Yet so many of these discussions are premised on prejudice rather than evidence that it is important to start from the facts.

It is now the case that 20 per cent of children in Britain today are growing up in families headed by a lone parent, while a growing proportion of babies – three in ten in 1992 – are being born outside marriage. However, contrary to popular myth, the proportion of very young women having children has been falling rapidly.

As those features emerge, it becomes clear that the attacks that have been launched recently on single parents – as if they were somehow the fount of crime and delinquency in our society – seems to owe more to misjudged political expediency than careful study of the facts.

Last year, in one of the most detailed scholastic investigations of the matter, David Utting concluded that 'the widely held assumption that two parents are automatically a better safeguard against delinquency is not supported by the evidence'.

Among the most relevant factors that Utting and his other researchers identified as contributing to childhood aggression and later delinquency were inadequate supervision and inconsistent discipline, parental indifference and neglect, conflict between parents, and parents who are or have been criminals themselves.

We shouldn't really be too surprised. The form of families may be changing but the needs of family members surely do not and, of course, children are affected by the attitudes and circumstances of their parents.

For parents, the opportunity to earn enough to keep their

children and themselves in comfort endures as surely as does the child's need for love, security, shelter and comfort.

Yet many of our country's children are being denied these most basic of supports. Even the most rudimentary right – the right to health – is not being guaranteed to all the youngest members of our society. A child born into a poor family is nearly twice as likely to die before the age of one as a child born into a well-off family. This gap actually widened during the 1980s.

It is these kind of insights that should prevent too many of society's ills being laid solely at the door of family breakdown. Families do not exist in a vacuum. They are, by definition, social institutions, and they reflect as well as shape the conditions of society itself.

And if too many of the families of today are not functioning to cater for the needs of all their members then we all pay a price. When children grow up in an environment of low opportunity and social instability they have to have an extraordinary degree of inherent strength in order to feel a sense of mutuality, of respect for each other and for society.

That is why the whole of society has a direct interest in and a direct obligation to increase opportunity and stability as a sustained matter of policy.

Of course most families are not breaking down, just as the great majority of juveniles are not criminal. But the breakdown in the bonds of family is intimately linked to the atomisation of society and community.

No one can afford that – not just because it represents a breakdown in what we conveniently, and rightly, regard to be essential moral conventions and codes, but also because it is just too expensive for any society to bear.

Even those who regard themselves to be on the New

Liberal Right of politics inadvertently acknowledge that when they produce their theories of the 'underclass'. It is an attempt to give a whole section a designation of irretrievable uselessness, to endow that group with complete blame for its own condition and, by such means, to exclude them from significance and to diminish their claims on the nation's resources.

It is a form of internal transportation which can, to some extent, obscure the fragmentation of society and, in the short term, give the impression that the public purse is being safeguarded.

But it isn't. Poverty, underperformance, low aspiration – especially when passed through generations – have multiplier effects. The millions who can fairly be described as 'disadvantaged' cannot be amputated from the rest of society. All that happens when basic ills are concealed or treated with quack remedies is that the costs and complexities of cure increase.

Employing strategies which deal with the sources of social ailment is not only morally enriching, therefore, it is materially rewarding.

A New Consensus

I confess that I have, at times, despaired about the possibility of building a political consensus for that view. Now, however, it does appear that within parts of the Conservative Party there has been a renewed interest in the place of community in our national, economic and social life.

The New Right's view of human beings as highly individualistic inhabitants of a market-place concerned solely with their own self-interest, and their endorsement of Jeremy Bentham's maxim that 'the community is a fictitious body, composed of . . . individual persons' has shaped Government policy-making for fifteen years.

Yet, as the results of those policies have become apparent, these views of the individual and the community have been revealed as a distorted and inadequate assessment of human nature on which to build an efficient economy and a just society and some Conservatives are beginning to acknowledge that.

The writings of John Gray, the Oxford philosopher previously identified with the ideas of the New Right, are, for instance, some indication of a philosophical reconsideration.

First in his study, *The Moral Foundations of Market Institutions*, published in 1992 and more recently in his pamphlet for the Social Market Foundation entitled *The Undoing of Conservatism*, Gray has argued that modern Conservatism's unquestioning adherence to the market, allied to continual denigration of the social institutions and traditions has left it ill-equipped to cope with the problems it has created.

And it should not therefore surprise political observers that as prominent a ministerial figure as the Chancellor of the Exchequer should recently have delivered a speech arguing that in his words 'community . . . had been in the lexicon of Conservatism for a long time . . . ' I would obviously advise anyone to sip a saline solution while listening to that, coming as it does from someone who is willing to levy 17.5 per cent on the fuel bills of the poorest people in the country. But it may be that words do father deeds and perhaps there are possibilities of a shift in policies.

I would certainly welcome that. But I do not think that it would be wise to depend upon it.

I want, therefore, to recommend a stronger approach: One that does not merely have the word 'community . . . in its lexicon' but has the concept of community at the core of its values and at the centre of actions and policies resulting from those values.

Being Interdependent   I have always adhered to the belief that the work of politicians must be informed by a view of human nature as well as a vision of society.

And for me, interdependence has always characterised the essence of the human condition.

Community is not, therefore, some abstract principle. It is the actualising of what is already common to all people – common hopes, common fears, and above all the common need for each other. And it also clearly goes beyond a geographic identity, or a static adherence to institutions or conduct rooted in the past.

Community is not so much created as discovered. People do not believe in Community any more than a fish believes in water. The feeling of Community is always already there, latent in our common humanity.

All of that should be self-evident. But as modern life is characterised increasingly as becoming inexorably more individualistic, it takes someone of rare insight to remind us of what we should already know.

Martin Luther King was such a man. In his time, he stated simply but accurately:

We are the everlasting debtors to known and unknown men and women. When we arise in the morning, we go into the bathroom where we reach for a sponge which is provided for us by a Pacific Islander. We reach for soap that is created for us by a European. Then at the table we drink coffee which is provided for us by a South American, or tea by a Chinese, or cocoa by a West African. Before we leave the house for our job we are already beholden to more than half of the world.

Understanding those realities of interdependence obviously does not exclude or diminish the importance of individualism. But it does mean comprehending the fact that societies that value and reward *only* individualism deny the true nature of humanity and cannot provide an adequate foundation for meeting the needs of their citizens.

Archbishop William Temple, who shared the same Christian faith as John Smith, acknowledged this. While he believed every person to be an individual, he wrote that our personalities were social, and as he put it 'only in their social relationships can men and women be persons'.

He went on to argue that this insight had great political importance, since these relationships flourished in the broad network of communities and fellowships. 'It is in these' he said, 'that the real wealth of human life consists.' **Understanding Community** And when we view community in this way – as an acknowledgment that as humans we are interdependent and therefore that our institutions and outlook should manifest that reality – we liberate the idea of community from old notions which regarded it exclusively as an expression of the all-powerful nation state in friendly guise.

Two consequences flow from such an understanding.

First: it becomes clear that community is not a threat to the freedom of individuals to realise their potential, rather it is the means through which personal freedom can be realised to the full.

Second: community is global.

Our interdependence extends throughout the world neighbourhood that is held together by shared purposes, mutual interests, related needs, and linked destinies.

The World Community

Truly the world is now an interdependent community in ways that are more tangible and immediate than ever before. That is why when a questioner asked Bob Geldof, 'Didn't anyone ever tell you that "Charity begins at home"?' he was honestly able to answer, 'Yes they did. And I agree with them. The world is my home.'

This sense of mutual interdependence clearly challenges us to address the pressing issue of the needs of the developing world – and by much more than charity alone. In addition, in a time which has seen the development of a truly global economy – with global firms, global technologies, global capital and global competition – economic integration emphasises the critical importance of more – and not less – co-operation between nations.

We are now aware as never before, for instance, that the industrial or agricultural practices on one continent will have environmental consequences extending far beyond its shores. There is increasing realisation that financial and trading terms imposed by one part of the world can so emaciate another part that they produce intensified poverty among the poor and contribute to recession for the rich.

And, in an age when the decisions to move capital around the globe are operated twenty-four hours a day, it is becoming ever clearer that the governments of nation states are increasingly impotent to address these changed circumstances on their own.

It is from this understanding of community as interdependence – as both a fact of modern life and also as a foundation for our personal ethics – that we can draw conclusions about what is the relevance of the idea of community in the modern world, why we should seek to further its effects and how the purposes of community can be cultivated through practical policies.

Strong Communities The task of government now is to refashion a new relationship between society and the individual, where rights and duties go hand in hand, where the aim of social action is to liberate the potential of individuals and where, in the words of Archbishop Tutu, 'It is clearly understood as the guiding maxim of policy that strong communities give birth to strong individuals and strong individuals give life to strong communities.'

It is only by acknowledging this public interest – by using the collective power of the community to allow individuals to realise their potential that we shall achieve such goals. By way of conclusion I will summarise what I believe that means in salient areas of policy.

Individual Opportunity First, it is essential that policies promote individual opportunity for *all* the members of our society.

The market alone, despite it dynamism, its freedom, its choices cannot do that. Indeed, the market does not exist to do it – and the sustained attempts to reduce provision of essential public services to a competitive lowest denominator provides daily proof of that in Britain.

Civilised communities are those in which fundamental individual opportunities of education, care and security are matters of rights, of equality of inputs. While there is always need for efficiency, probity and financial responsibility in the provision of those opportunities, such provision must be a matter of entitlement, not of trading in a social stock exchange.

If a society departs from such an understanding, the result is not only injustice, it is incompetence too.

It is, for instance, no mere coincidence that the most

competitive modern economies in the world are also those
which have invested most in the nourishment of the abilities
of whole generations instead of leaving achievement to
accidents of birth or fortune. That is merely one practical
instance of the way in which the literal application of ideas
of community spirit and individual opportunity are mutual
servants. And what is distinctive about the societies which
have made such broad, high quality provision is not that
they have forsaken the market. It is that they have simply
discriminated between what the market reasonably could and
should do and what it should not be relied upon to do.

Social Cohesion   In order to achieve the proper synthesis of
community provision and individual opportunity, of course,
a society should have a system of contributions and benefits
which fosters social cohesion: It would be foolish and
unrealistic to ignore the fact that taxpayers at all levels
of income have varying degrees of self-interest and that,
for many, a net income in the hand is worth a lot of future
opportunity, health care and retirement provision in the
bush. I believe, therefore, that there is now an urgent need
to increase transparency in taxation so that the link between
the level of payment that goes in and the standard of provision
that comes out is clear and comprehensible. In the case of the
Health and Community Care Services, for instance, there
should be a specific named tax that would fund provision and
replace part of the so called 'standard rate'. By that means,
the great majority of people who, for a mixture of personal
and altruistic reasons, give a particular value to these services
can relate their demand for high standards and availability of
provision to their willingness to make collective payment.

There must also, obviously, be a basic fairness in taxation.
We therefore cannot continue to have a taxation system that
permits the profound inequity of the very rich being able to

use tax loopholes to ensure that they pay no direct taxation, while pensioners through their fuel bills are expected to pay much more in regressive indirect taxation.

In terms of law and order there is no constructive crime-defeating purpose to be served in John Major's 'Understanding a little less and condemning a little more'. While criminals must very obviously be detected, tried and punished, it is clear that without effective efforts of prevention and rehabilitation the best that can be hoped for is a slower rise in crime, never a sustained reduction in the rates of crime. Where there is an environment of idleness, lack of opportunity and little hope of achievement, self-esteem fades. When that occurs, lack of respect or consideration for others follows close behind. It then becomes impossible for interdependence to be recognised or for community to thrive. Whatever crime-fighting systems are developed, therefore, it is crucially important to follow policies that increase the possibility of preventing or deterring the conditions which create the *first* crime – and 'understanding a little more' must be part of that process.

Fostering Personal Responsibility In social policy we need an approach that seeks to foster rather than replace personal responsibility. Guaranteeing the people who are out of work full opportunities to train and to volunteer would be a start to such progress. Providing a hand up rather than merely a hand-out is, in the short term, possibly more expensive. But there can be no doubt about its financial, economic and social benefit in the medium and longer term. There are those, of course, who say that strategies which emphasise the value of training and supplementary education are 'well intended, but take too long to work to be of real value'. I've been listening to them saying it for well over a decade. I can only reflect ruefully on the fact that, if the action had started when they first said it, the improvement would have been obvious for years.

My belief in community, indeed my most basic motives for being active in politics derive now, as they always have, from my conviction that men and women are primarily social beings and that human nature is, in Aneurin Bevan's words, 'at least as much cooperative as it is competitive'.

Idealism, I readily acknowledge, does make a contribution to that conviction. But it is fuelled mainly by realism. We are so frequently told that 'human nature' is instinctively and irretrievably cruel, selfish, exploitive and deceitful that opinions to the contrary can sound naïve. But experience as well as instinct has long persuaded me that if compassion, generosity and honesty were *really* departures from the norm it is they – and *not* the manifestations of evil – that would fill the headlines. This feeling does not make me a physical or a political pacifist or provide me with permanent rose-tinted contact lenses. Far from it. The knowledge that evil is memorable, sensational, *newsworthy* because it is abnormal, eccentric, a departure from the main flow of human nature, does, however, give me optimism in the cause of community.

That, by itself, is clearly not enough – hence the need which I have always felt to engage in political activity. 'For evil to triumph' said Burke, 'it is only necessary for good men to do nothing' – and goodness of that kind, I have always felt, I could well do without.

The task, therefore, is to try to secure different social and economic arrangements so that I, and my fellow human beings, here and in the rest of the world, can derive the full benefits of community.

Countless others are, of course, engaged in that task: They manifest it through their altruism as volunteers and professionals, through their practical concern for the poor and suffering, for the environment, for security in the future. They show it through their understanding of the integration and interdependence of economies and peoples and in a multitude of other ways.

The efforts are disparate, they are often demonstrated as single-issue commitments and it is probable that, as a result, the full combined impact of the work, the contributions, the ideas is diminished to some extent.

Common Endeavour At its best, democratic politics exist to make up for that shortfall in potential, not by trying to ride a rainbow of diverse concerns or offering easy promises to meet the multiplicity of needs and demands. But by reflecting the values which inspire those who seek the betterment of others and, by so doing, demonstrate their active belief in common endeavour, common responsibility, common interest in the quality and the fate of their society and their world.

Consistent pursuit of policies based on such ethics will probably not bring speedy advance on all fronts. But it is much more likely to achieve gradual and perceptible progress for individuals and for societies than is the fragmentation and isolation that is the alternative.

For that practical reason, it is essential that ours is a country with a sense of community.

It is unlikely to enable us to build heaven on earth – but it is surely the best means that we shall have for preventing hell on earth.

BIBLIOGRAPHICAL NOTE

1 Matthew Arnold, *Mixed Essays* (Smith Elder & Co, London, 1879).

10

What a Waste

*Chris Bryant trained for ordination at Oxford and in
Buenos Aires, and first worked as a curate in High
Wycombe and as Youth Chaplain to the Bishop of
Peterborough. In 1991 he went to work for the Labour
Party as Frank Dobson's agent, and subsequently as
Local Government Development Officer. He is Chief
Whip on Hackney Council, and has been Chair of
the Christian Socialist Movement since 1993. He edited*
Reclaiming the Ground.

When John Smith died perhaps the most common feeling,
expressed by those who knew him and those who never met
him alike, was a sense of frustration at a life cut short and
of a lost opportunity. For John Smith's style of leading the
Labour Party had already shown the strength of purpose he
would bring to bear as a supremely effective and principled
Prime Minister. He came across as one who knew what was
required of him, one who held to his beliefs passionately and
yet with generosity of intellect, and one who dearly wanted to
have the opportunity to serve his country. That he was never
to serve in that highest office will always feel a waste.

The theme is not a new one, of course. For Ian Dury sang the song 'What a waste' in the seventies, and it is still a resonant theme for the nineties, for if anything marks the political landscape of modern Britain it is the frustrated sense of wasted talents, opportunities and materials, squandered through an economic system and a political ideology that sees no absolute value to unleashing potential. We are a talented nation, endowed with a great capacity for invention, for artistic endeavour, for co-operative venture and for hard work, but we are led to underachieve by an economic system that only values cold market outcomes, and a political system that has regard only to the already economically active. What a waste.

Efficiency

Yet the concept of efficiency must be at the heart of any understanding of politics. For we know that the resources of the earth, or of an individual nation, are finite. The world's carbon fuels will not last for ever. The rain forests of the Amazon, the earth's natural lungs, cannot produce indefinite quantities of hardwood. The earth cannot bio-degrade the rubbish of our consumer society at an indefinitely accelerating pace. The capacity of the planet to absorb pollution is not infinite. So a key element of any political economy must be the best and most efficient use of our resources. First of all this must mean reducing the waste with which we daily fill our rubbish bins. Where waste cannot be reduced, it should be re-used. Where it cannot be re-used it should be recycled, and where it cannot be recycled it should be dealt with in a way that is most environmentally efficient, such as by incineration with heat generation being used productively. Our economic revival must be based on a principle of sustainability.

For even the land we live on has been contaminated by a lengthy history of old tips, abandoned factories and polluted waterways. The vast potential development site of King's Cross is just such an area, where what could be a site for homes, for leisure, for light industry, is presently a derelict wasteland. Large tracts of our inner cities feel less like secure environments and more like industrial refugee sites, where factories have made their environmentally irresponsible mark, and having writ, moved on. Which is why the present government's addiction to road-building, largely due to their being hi-jacked by the road lobbying group, at the expense of public transport, is as keen an example of the careless disregard for matters of environmental efficiency as there could be. For the ludicrous determination to build roads through green space after green space belies any commitment to the long-term future of the world economy.

At the same time it is important to note that the wasting of resources is not just a casual outcome of the present system. There is indeed a causal link which means that waste has become one of the present government's list of achievements. It is as if Dickens' office of 'How Not to Do It' were still in operation. For over the last few years we have seen a dramatic series of incidents of waste that have followed directly from government policy and failure to provide open government. Take the British Library, now under construction on Euston Road, next to St Pancras railway station. It was meant to be finished in 1988, at a cost of £115.8 million. There is presently no expected finish date, and the budget has been increased to £450 million. Even so it will only provide 130 more reading desks than the present library, and will not be able to house the full collection. Take the Regional Development Corporations with millions of pounds of taxpayers' money wasted in the fraud and incompetence of the unelected state.

And finally take the government's record on housing, with 765,000 empty homes in 1993, representing 15 per cent of its stock, compared to only 70,909 empty homes in the local government sector, representing 1.9 per cent of their total.

The Nation's Resources

So the goal of efficiency must be the key to politics. J. M. Keynes put it this way: 'The political problem of mankind is to combine three things: economic efficiency, social justice and individual liberty.'[1] Nye Bevan went further, to argue that 'the language of priorities is the religion of socialism', and this is exactly true. The political endeavour is to ensure the best use of our resources, and these resources are manifold: financial, material, human, cultural. For the resources available to the economy and to society are not simply the raw materials, or indeed the manufactured goods, that are harboured within our territory. Our heritage, our cultural identity, and the richness of our artistic life is just as vital – especially so in a nation where tourism is one of our major industries. Here it is a matter of real concern that our investment in that heritage is so poor and unplanned, in large measure abandoned to private patronage. Country villages are in danger of losing their post offices through privatisation and therefore their local shops. The larger towns have lost out to the out-of-town hypermarkets, leaving once popular market squares with boarded-up shops and a dead-end economy. London presently has more theatres 'dark' than at any other time since the war. Indeed it is only local government, in co-operation with private industry, that has been able to force the pace in the tourism industry, with such innovations as the Glasgow's Miles Better campaign followed by the adoption of Glasgow as Europe's City of Culture. Many of our major cities, adopting the One Per Cent for Art principle, have not only enlivened their cultural heritage but brought private investment into the local economy, revitalising areas like the docks in Gloucester and Liverpool.

War

The greatest waste of all, however, is the waste of human resources, and the keenest example of this is the waste of war. So from the First World War the image of the young who died in such enormous numbers in the trenches has still a peculiar potency:

> These laid the world away; poured out the red
> Sweet wine of youth; gave up the years to be
> Of work and joy, and that unhoped serene,
> That men call age; and those that would have been,
> Their sons, they gave, their immortality.

> Rupert Brooke, 'The Dead'

Every war has blighted the lives of the young, and the theatre, the cinema and television all know the power of the symbolism, for the death of a young person 'before their time' has the emotive strength to remind us of all our own unfulfilled ambitions. A. E. Housman put it in another way:

> Here dead lie we because we did not choose
> To live and shame the land from which we sprung.
> Life to be sure, is nothing much to lose;
> But young men think it is, and we were young.

113

So it is right that all politicians should be cautious about war. Even the Republican leader Herbert Hoover acknowledged it: 'Older men declare war. But it is youth who must fight and die. And it is youth who must inherit the tribulation, the sorrow, and the triumphs that are the aftermath of war.'[2] Yet America crippled itself only a few years later in Vietnam, where the average age of US fatalities was nineteen. The Falklands war too saw many seventeen-year-old Argentinians from the provincial towns of the north die on cold wet mountains. And in 1994, the sight of countless thousands murdered in Rwanda, and the constant images of death in the former Yugoslavia, are a vivid reminder of both the real value of human life, with all its possibilities, and the cheapness of human life in a time of war.

Yet Britain's economy depends on war. Many of our industries only flourish when there is the possibility of selling arms to one or other, or preferably both, sides of a conflict. Throughout the eighties the government continued to allow sales of arms and intelligence materials to Chile and other dictatorships in Latin America.

Peace

Socialism, however, has always had a ferocious distrust of war. Thus Ernie Bevin: 'There never has been a war yet which, if the facts had been put calmly before the ordinary folk, could not have been prevented . . . The common man, I think, is the great protection against war.'[3] Kier Hardie struggled hard against the First World War, seeing it as totally inimical to the real aspirations of the working class. George Lansbury too was an overt pacifist in his approach, a line followed through into the Peace Movement, the Campaign for Nuclear Disarmament,

Christian CND and the work of many activists on the Christian Left.

Yet many of us would consider ourselves to be 'not quite pacifists'. For there are instances, at least hypothetical ones, in which we would fight. Thus the declaration of Camillo Torres, the Latin-American priest who struggled for liberation theology: that it was impossible for a Catholic not to be a revolutionary might be an over-statement, but none the less there are cases in which I would be prepared to take up arms, despite all the moral ambiguities, despite the probable inequities, despite the logical folly of war. For it is not that war is ever justified, but that the alternative, which may be genocide or oppression or murder, is against every principle of our common humanity, and must be opposed with all our strength, with all our mind and with all our soul.

So the major task of international policy must be the pursuit of the common good and of peace. And a socialist government must always have as one of its key elements the establishment of the best possible relations between the nations. Yet we must also maintain a close vigil over the human rights of those in other nations, keen to use our international clout in the pursuit of peace. As Franklin D. Roosevelt said in his inaugural address in 1933, 'In the field of world polity, I would dedicate this nation to the policy of the good neighbour.'[4] We live in a world where we have to accept responsibility for one another.

For above all, peace without justice is not peace, just as justice without peace is not justice. They are interdependent, or as it is put in the Bible, 'Justice and Peace shall kiss one another'. Peace with justice is our goal, within a society that truly harnesses all the skills and endless possibilities that human beings can be capable of. As Donald Soper put it, 'Peace is the fruit of justice and can grow on no other tree.'[5]

The waste of people that war not only tolerates but demands can never feed the needs of the world.

The Lives of the Young

Furthermore the battle against waste is not just against the blight that pollution and war represent. It must also in Britain today focus very specifically on the lives of young people, both because it is into their hands that we shall commend the future, and also because it is their strength that we must harness. As Disraeli put it, 'We live in an age when to be young and indifferent can no longer be synonymous. We must prepare for the coming hour. The claims of the Future are represented by suffering millions; and the Youth of a Nation are the trustees of Posterity.'[6]

Yet the talents and abilities of many of our young people today are undoubtedly wasted. Unemployment, under-employment, poor access to further and higher education, homelessness, poor public transport and expensive leisure facilities – all these mean in our rural and city areas that teenagers and children are often experiencing their first blasts of adulthood without any real chance to succeed, and that success is measured anyway in terms of competing with someone else and winning.

So above all, Britain needs today a sense that the wasted opportunities and talent of young people, and not so young people, can be turned around. We need to feel as keen a sense of outrage about unemployment, poor educational opportunities and all that hampers the fullest possible development of young people as we do about the waste that is war. As William Temple argued, 'we are challenged to find a social order which provides employment, steadily and generally, and our consciences should be restive till we succeed.'[7]

Real Concerns

In a recent Youth Crime Audit in the London Borough of Hackney, by far the most common reply to the question 'What do you worry about?' put to young people was 'Getting a job'. This came just ahead of concerns about doing well at school and one's own personal safety. The survey goes on, 'Leaving school or waiting to leave school having achieved "nothing" seemed to be a prime formative experience for the more alienated young people.' Clearly it is amongst these young people, who perceive themselves to have achieved nothing when it comes to the first major hurdle of adulthood, that the dangers of youth crime are strongest. For Hackney has among the highest levels of youth crime in London, especially in terms of car crime, theft and burglary, as well as drug-related offending. And at the same time Hackney scores highly on all the risk factors known to be associated with juvenile offending, particularly family stress, youth unemployment and housing difficulties.

Yet over recent years, throughout the country, local communities have seen all the various forms of youth provision known to ameliorate the rate of juvenile offending cut back. Where there used to be a couple of uniformed youth organisations, a church youth group, alternative educational provision for excluded children, play schemes and cheap leisure facilities, now there may only be one local youth club. With no statutory requirement to provide a youth service, and with the decline of many of the church-based voluntary youth organisations, there has been a dramatic cut in the wider youth service. Youth-work programmes have been an easy and an early casualty in enforced local government cut-backs under the capping regime.

So we are left with dramatic under-provision, both in the

inner cities and in the rural areas, for young people. Where this is matched with high levels of local deprivation, there has been a seemingly inexorable rise in levels of delinquency. Truancy task forces are over-stretched and feel they are simply engaged in an act of containment, whilst the youth service simply lurches from one round of savings to another round of cuts. At the same time the formal education system is in disarray following a decade of conflict with the government, and an incessant demand from successive Ministers for new procedures, new tests, new curricula, new financial systems.

Redressing the Waste

Yet the answer must be twofold. First, government has to understand the dramatic need to create opportunities for employment for young people that are more than dead-end training schemes. This has to be accompanied by locally-based employment development work including skill training and providing help with setting up a small business, but in the end is a macro-economic issue relating to the government's real investment in the economy. This also has to include advice and help for young people with housing as there is a clear link between overcrowding and youth homelessness and drug-related crime. Young single homeless cannot simply be left either at the end of the queue or out in the cold when it comes to housing provision.

Secondly, we need a climate of schooling that is geared towards fostering a sense of achievement in all young people, starting as early as possible. Homework clubs and similar support mechanisms, as well as well-resourced alternative educational provision for children excluded from school, are vital. Detached youth work with young people on the street, as well as youth clubs and organisations from the voluntary sector, integrated with the school service, can also play a key role in assisting the fullest development of individuals.

Education

For the development of Britain's young people should not solely be seen as the successful pushing through the system of so many young faces. What we must be engaged in is giving every young person the greatest possible chance in life to achieve. This is not just a question of acquiring facts. Anatole France described the task: 'The whole art of teaching is only the art of awakening the natural curiosity of young minds for the purpose of satisfying it afterwards; and curiosity itself can be vivid and wholesome only in proportion as the mind is contented and happy.'[8] In other words the educational process will only be valuable in so far as the young people themselves have secure homes to live in, know where their next meal is coming from, are free from fear of bullying and abuse, and enjoy a happy family life. Not all of this can be legislated for, of course. After all the government cannot tell us all to be happy. What it can do is create the social environment in which everyone can realise the fruits of their own abilities, a genuinely educational environment. The simple stuffing of minds full of 'facts, facts, facts' as in Dickens' *Hard Times* will barely suffice for the training necessary for the art of living into the twenty-first century when technological advance will rapidly require new training of us all every decade. What we truly need from our educational system is the ability to instill in young people an appetite for knowledge, the desire to comprehend, and an understanding of their own value and

119

significance. Over and above this young people need an environment in which they can acquire the personal skills that they will need to survive in society, as well as a moral grounding.

So it is absolutely essential that education must be at the very heart of any democratic socialist endeavour. Education is the one great equaliser of the human condition, the balance wheel of the social machinery, and if it is dislodged so as to perpetuate inequality it will have lost its purpose. Martin Luther King was right to see education as the key to the possibility of racial harmony, and democratic socialists can ignore the real educational needs of our young people at their peril. Presently our education system is under-resourced and over-burdened with bureaucracy. Our teachers often feel unfulfilled after years of oppositional politics from the government. Our young people under-perform, and we are left with an educational climate of permanent upheaval rather than steady progress, in the midst of which we squander the best of our talents and leave many to fend for themselves, especially in areas of multiple deprivation. Wasted educational opportunities, wasted life chances and wasted potential. Yet for the future what we should seek to achieve is full nursery education for all who want it; real formal educational opportunities that foster achievement at whatever level; a secure grounding in the personal skills that social living requires; real training in work skills; rapid integration of technological advance with educational methods; a statutory extra-curricular youth service releasing personal, artistic, creative skills that cannot be accommodated at school; and all this within a social framework that guarantees for every child a secure home, freedom from violence and abuse, access to learning, healthy food, clean water and adequate clothing.

Clear Choices

At the turn of every century each nation seeks to reinvent itself, and as we approach the new millennium Britain should do so with fervour. For we have clear choices which are really moral choices: a society that decides to let each person fight his or her own way through the vicissitudes of life, with the market system determining provision of health care, education, youth service and of course, employment, or a nation that understands itself to have a corporate responsibility to foster the potential of its individual citizens and local communities, to build opportunities for them to succeed and to safeguard their periods of weakness. Neutrality at such a time has to be as inexcusable as it was for Dante, who placed the fence-sitters in the hottest section of the Inferno.

No, the task ahead of us is clear, to rebuild the wastelands and to create a social and political environment that uses all the resources that are available to us efficiently and for the common good. We shall be able to determine whether we are achieving anything like that goal by the way we live up to the aims William Temple set in 1942:

1. Every child should find itself a member of a family housed with decency and dignity, so that it may grow up as a member of that basic community in a happy fellowship unspoilt by underfeeding or overcrowding, by dirty or drab surroundings or by mechanical monotony of environment.
2. Every child should have the opportunity of an education till years of maturity, so planned as to allow for his peculiar aptitudes and make possible their full development.[9]

121

While the talents and potential of our young people are wasted on the sidelines of the economy, poorly educated for a modern technological age, ill-prepared for adulthood and left with no expectation of work, we shall never know what they, or we as a nation, are capable of, and we shall have failed the future generations.

Our final words, however, must be ones of hope, for the task of rebuilding our communities, the political task of national renewal, cannot simply be the work of those who have already tried to run the country for so many years. It must now become the task of youth. For, as Robert Kennedy argued,

> Our answer is the world's hope; it is to rely on youth. The cruelties and obstacles of this swiftly changing planet will not yield to obsolete dogmas and outworn slogans. It cannot be moved by those who cling to a present which is already dying, who prefer the illusion of security to the excitement of danger. It demands the qualities of youth: not a time of life but a state of mind, a temper of the will, a quality of the imagination, a predominance of courage over timidity, of the appetite for adventure over the love of ease.[10]

BIBLIOGRAPHICAL NOTES

1 J. M. Keynes in *Social Christianity – a reader*, ed. J. Atherton (SPCK, London, 1994).
2 H. Hoover, speech at Republican National Convention, Chicago, 27 June 1944.
3 *Hansard*, 23 November 1945.
4 *F. D. Roosevelt, Inaugural Address, 4 March 1933*.

5 *Cited in Soperisms*, ed. B. Frost, (New World Publications, London, 1993).

6 B. Disraeli, *Sybil* (OUP, Oxford, 1981; first published 1845), final sentence.

7 W. Temple, *Christianity and the social order* (Penguin, London, 1942).

8 A. France, *The crime of Sylvestre Bonnard*, in *The Works of Anatole France*, trs. Lafcadio Hearn, vol. 1 part 2, ch 4, (1860), p. 198; (Bodley Head, London, 1924).

9 W. Temple, *op. cit.*

10 R. F. Kennedy, Day of Affirmation speech, University of Cape Town, 6 June 1966.

11

The Task of Politics

Terry Wynn was brought up and educated in Wigan, and entered the Merchant Navy as an engineer. Subsequent engineering work led him to take an MSc at Salford University. He was a Wigan councillor for eleven years, and was Chair of Economic Development. In 1989 he was elected Member of the European Parliament for Merseyside East, and was re-elected in May 1994 for Merseyside East and Wigan. He is a Methodist local preacher and member of the Christian Socialist Movement.

In March 1993 John Smith said, 'Let us not underestimate the desire, which I believe is growing in our society, for a politics based on principle.' There can be few in Britain today, whether they have an interest in politics or not, who would argue with him. The extended recession, the deep disillusionment with the government over broken election promises, the apparent 'economy with the truth' in the Scott Inquiry, the soaring rate of crime, the extension of political patronage and the lining of senior managers' pockets in the newly privatised industries have left us a nation ill at ease with our government, deeply mistrustful, in many cases, of all forms of authority.

Yet the response to John Smith's premature death, depriving Britain and the Labour Party of one of its greatest leaders, betokened above all the desire for just such a politics. Britain is looking to its leaders for a very radical social and political renewal that is based on principle.

Principles & Politics

Yet it is dangerous to talk of principle in politics without defining the parameters. For whilst it is easy to bandy words such as honesty and integrity, it is more difficult to tie down exactly what these words mean in the political arena. By the very nature of political democracy those who put themselves up for election, our 'politicians', affect honesty, integrity, even humility. Quite rightly it is rare for a politician to question the personal integrity of another, just as it would be wholly inappropriate for one person to question the integrity of another's faith, simply because one disagreed with the political conclusions it had brought them to. The dictum 'judge not, that ye be not judged' should be written on the hearts of all who enter politics, whether their judgmentalism assaults the party opposition or the convenient scapegoats of society.

Furthermore the trustworthiness of an individual will always be impossible to gauge without the evidence of their acts. Shakespeare put it well in *Macbeth*, when Duncan, having been betrayed by one of his most loyal henchmen, says

> There's no art
> To find the mind's construction in the face;
> He was a gentleman on whom I built
> An absolute trust.'

Macbeth, 1.IV.11–14

This is precisely how Britain seems to feel today, bruised by disillusionment, and conscious of a government whose primary aim seems to be self-preservation. The experience of the last general election, with the two headline Conservative advertising slogans of 'Labour's tax bombshell' and 'You can't trust Labour', rapidly followed by one of the most audacious and flagrant turnarounds, with the greatest ever tax hike in history and a series of other broken promises, has undoubtedly left the electorate politically traumatised. In such a context the word 'politician' has become a term of abuse, and few are surprised when a senior member of the government admits that it is necessary for Ministers to lie.

So it was that when John Smith died, and people either discovered for the first time or realised what they already knew, that John Smith himself, in the words of Thomas Hardy, 'was a good man, and he did good things', and that in fact all politicians are humans, no more no less, a different force came into play.

For though modern elections, even at a local level, will have their defining moments determined by the press and media, the real political debate is one of ideas. What will affect the more fundamental social swing will be not a beauty contest for the most apparently trustworthy, but a tussle over the contours of the principles and values that Britain wants to see embodied in its political system.

The New Right

Yet there are those who would have us believe that a politics based on principle is at best impracticable and at worst either irrelevant or improper. Thus Nigel Lawson in 1993 argued that 'all that is left to socialism is the moral high ground' and Peter Lilley asserted earlier this year, 'I don't think a political party should be the source of a moral vision.'[1] Both of them fundamentally underestimate the task of politics, which is not only to govern and to lead, but to frame the political agenda in such a way that people feel at ease with their government. As John Smith said, 'Let me assert my profound conviction that politics ought to be a moral activity.'[2] Or, as Harold Wilson put it, 'This party is a moral crusade or it is nothing.'[3]

The Roots of our Principles

Others, of course, would quite correctly argue that Britain is a secular society, nominally Christian but in essence pluralist, and that to impose any moral system on society through government intervention would be wrong. Yet the task of developing and propounding a politics based on our common social principles, rather than the simple free-for-all of modern-day Conservatism, must be key to any socialist endeavour. For the protection of minorities, the fuller development of the role of many of our minority communities, and the fundamental respect for the freedom of the individual: all these can only truly stem from a moral understanding of the role of government. Of course no political party or individual politician that sought to impose one set of moral values – or indeed one religion – on another should be worthy of election in a democratic pluralist society. So it is not that we should wish to rebuild Christendom – that way the madness of religious oppression and fundamentalism lies. Our aim, however, must be to establish our political agenda on the sturdy foundations of our common social values. Britain is, and I hope will remain, a secular society with a strong Christian tradition, and the Labour Movement exactly mirrors it.

William Temple understood the role of faith within

politics: 'The Church must announce Christian principles and point out where the existing social order at any time is in conflict with them. It must then pass on to Christian citizens, acting in their civic capacity, the task of re-shaping the existing order in closer conformity to the principles.'[4]

For some of us, and for me personally, those principles are rooted in Christian faith. For others they will stem from a different faith, or from the sheer force of their own reason, unallied to any faith. For the vast majority it will come from what they quite simply know to be right and true. The principles will be the same, though their roots may differ.

What are our Central Principles?

The Material   First is the belief that human life is not a series of compartmentalised sections that can be dealt with separately and without reference to each other. The physical, the emotional, the intellectual and the spiritual may be separate aspects of our experience, but they each depend upon each other, connect with each other. Thus William Temple, the left-of-centre Archbishop of Canterbury during the Second World War, said, 'Christianity is the most materialistic of all great religions,'[5] and so, in the proper sense of the term, should be our democratic socialism. For it is impossible to atomise our humanity and our political endeavour. Material needs matter, and so do intellectual needs.

Yet many would argue that all that counts is the moral fibre of the individual. From this fundamental belief comes the assertion that it is only the 'deserving poor' that we should value, and let the 'undeserving poor' care for themselves. Apologists for the New Right such as Charles Murray go on to state that the welfare state itself is the cause of a growing

129

'underclass', populated by 'barbarians' and 'illegitimate babies'. By a systematic logical inversion, the meeting of real need in areas of the inner cities, according to the Right, actually creates the problems of society. Murray completes the logical circle by arguing 'I want to re-introduce the notion of blame' so that the poor are forced to stand on their own two feet.

Yet for democratic socialists two things count. First real material need, especially the need for food, clean water, health care, secure accommodation, an income; these wear away at the soul and insidiously weaken communities and families. The Commission on Social Justice's first report, 'The Justice Gap', cited some of the effects of such grinding poverty: 'I get so depressed. Kids on at me all the time for this and that, and I know they need it but I just haven't got the money. Then I end up bashing them, then I sit by myself and cry.'[6] (*The Justice Gap*, IPPR, p. 23).

Secondly, all humans aspire to more than simply meeting their physical needs. Security, personal fulfilment, satisfaction, dignity, self-respect, love – all these are personal needs that must play just as important a role in the political agenda for democratic socialists as the basic need for food and air. The dictum 'Man cannot live by bread alone' must mean that our individual and communal aspirations are part of the weft and warp of our humanity. Poverty is the dry rot, in many of our cities and rural areas, that destroys the building blocks of our society, its families, its local communities.

So the art is to create a political system that can tackle the root causes of poverty, can meet the needs of the poor, and simultaneously tackles dependency and develops real opportunity for all, through education, training, employment, to escape poverty. For our ambition as democratic socialists must be not just a crusade against material poverty, but a systematic and consistent deploying of every effort to ensure that every individual, every family, every community enjoys the full fruits of a fulfilling life.

Which means that if humanity is not a series of independent aspects, material, intellectual, spiritual, but a single integrated whole, we need a political system that responds to humanity in an integrated way. I am struck in particular by the failure of the welfare system to treat people as individuals. One department requires one form, another requires another and even in local government the system is often so complicated, with separate offices for every function of the authority, that the individual, unless one is a professional welfare expert, is permanently foxed. Thus too it must still be unhelpful that the state recognises young people as responsible adults at such a wide variety of ages, through from ten, when they may be tried in a juvenile court, to twenty-one, when they may stand for election.

Furthermore national government rarely integrates its work. We know that one aspect of policy affects another, and it is folly to abstract any one concern from the rest. Thus the economic performance of this country depends on the skills and aptitudes of its workforce. That in turn depends on both the health of the nation and on the educational standards and opportunities afforded our young people, as well as the immediate availability of training for those already in work. Educational performance, of course, also depends both on good schooling and parental support, but also on a secure home-life, in a decent home with parents who themselves feel part of society. That we have forced our economy into supporting for so long an unacceptable level of unemployment is not only a devastating judgment on the government which saw it as the 'inevitable cost of low inflation'. It also shows the ability of Conservatism to atomise society and to fail to

131

make the connections. Unemployment costs the economy, it wastes talent, it weakens families, it destroys children's hopes and it ruins the economy of the future, condemning us to a low-wage, low-skills, low-hope decline.

Optimism   Our second principle must be that our understanding of humanity is essentially optimistic. Of course we bear the marks of sinfulness, and we are all capable of self-interest. Indeed self-interest and self-preservation are amongst the strongest reflexes we have. But two things need to be remembered. First, those instincts for self-preservation do not only function for the individual. As often as not we seek to preserve not just ourselves but our families, our friends, our local community. Self-interest can often serve the common good.

Furthermore humanity is not just instinctively greedy and self-interested. We are capable of enormous acts of altruism, the concepts of duty and sacrifice are close to the heart of every human culture, and humans are endowed with enormous capacity for invention, courage, independence of thought, compassion, generosity and determination.

And this matters because Conservatism argues that because we are fallen we need a system that caters for our sinful nature. Socialism, it is argued, would work were it not for the fact that without the totally unhindered opportunity for self-advancement there would be no invention, the entrepreneurial spirit would fade. Competition is what makes the world go round, and any interference in that fundamental truth will only lead to harm.

But the truth is that the sinfulness humanity is capable of is more commonly turned to greed than to sloth. St Basil said, 'If each one would take that which is sufficient for one's needs, leaving what is in excess to those in distress, no one would be rich, no one would be poor.' So it is undoubtedly true that people of faith are called to a special lifestyle of generosity and 'live simply that others may simply live'. We are, however, naturally acquisitive, and the consumer world in which we live depends on us succumbing to the pressures of advertising, buying what we do not need, wanting what we could do without. For good and for less good reasons we seek to better ourselves, to enable our children to enjoy greater opportunities than we ourselves did. We seek to build up savings in order to protect our financial security when we are no longer economically active. And we hope to earn more in our middle age than in our youth.

All these are natural instincts which a political system can only seek to deny at a cost to its credibility. Yet the worst excesses of our consumer economy do need reigning in. It must be offensive that those at the top of the wage bracket have enjoyed in recent years not only a phenomenal tax holiday but also the most marked pay increases, way in excess of inflation, whilst the majority, especially those in the public sector, have enjoyed the slimmest of annual pay rises.

So our optimism about human nature will be tempered by a realistic estimation of the greed and selfishness of which we are capable.

Our Social Nature Our third principle is that we believe that humanity is by its very nature social. John Donne, the poet and Dean of St Paul's, put it at its fullest,

No man is an Iland, intire of it selfe; every man is a peece of the Continent, a part of the maine; if a clod bee washed away by the Sea, Europe is the lesse, as well as if a Promontorie were, as well as if a Mannor of thy friends or of thine owne were; any mans death diminishes me, because I am involved in Mankinde; And therefore never send to know for whom the bell tolls; it tolls for thee.[7]

133

That is to say the pure unbridled individualism of a *laissez-faire* market economy will not meet the real aspirations of our humanity. We are born to be our brothers' and our sisters' keepers, and it is as morally offensive now as it was in first-century Palestine that people should cross over to the other side of the road when they see a person in need. We have a personal responsibility for one another.

J. B. Priestley's play *An Inspector Calls*, in its somewhat hackneyed way, makes this very point. For once the Inspector has made his elaborate enquiries of the Birling family, each of whom is subtly implicated in the death of a young woman called Eva Smith, he delivers his apocalyptic message:

> But just remember this. One Eva Smith has gone – but there are millions and millions of Eva Smiths . . . still left with us, with their lives, their hopes and fears, their suffering, and chances of happiness, all intertwined with our lives, with what we think and say and do. We don't live alone. And I tell you that the time will soon come when, if men will not learn that lesson, then they will be taught it in fire and blood and anguish.[8]

Yet we have had fifteen years in which the message has been that it is right and proper solely to look after *Numero Uno*, that individual fulfilment and success is the sole element in our personal responsibility. As long as we are doing well, then that is enough.

The cost of such an ethic is immense. For these same years have seen a radical acceleration in the crime rate, a devastation of the communal life of many of our towns and villages, let alone our cities, and a sharpening of the divide between the rich and the poor. Pius XI's words from 1931 might equally well be used today, 'The ultimate consequences of the individualist spirit in economic life are these: free competition has destroyed itself; economic dictatorship has supplanted the free market; unbridled ambition for power has likewise succeeded greed for gain; economic life has become tragically hard, inexorable and cruel.'[9]

Furthermore we know that we are social beings, for otherwise we should not bother with other people. Solitary confinement is rightly the worst punishment there is because it deprives us of one of the most important aspects of our very selves, our need to communicate, to be with others, to live in society. As Temple put it 'Man [sic] is naturally and incurably social',[10] or as Archbishop William Laud put it in his sermon before the King on 19 June 1621, 'If any man be so addicted to his private, that he neglect the common state, he is void of the sense of piety and wisheth peace and happiness to himself in vain. For whoever he be, he must live in the body of the Commonwealth . . . ' Community is central then to our Christian understanding, for not only did the early disciples 'hold every thing in common', but the social gospel of Jesus was a constant attempt to undo the barriers of prejudice and narrow-mindedness that isolated the individual.

More than that, of course, is our personal and social need for community, by which we understand what A. H. Halsey has called *koinonia* or the 'fellowship of sharing'. For wherever we share an interest, a home, a village, a faith, a culture, a democratic system, we are inevitably set within a community. We can choose to ignore that community, just as it can choose to ignore us, and we can choose to work towards strengthening those community ties, or weakening them. What we cannot do is deny that communal life is an inevitable part of our internal geography.

And few would argue that our communities have been

135

weakened over recent years. We hear of elderly people dying and being found only after several years. We know of tower blocks and streets where neighbours never exchange a greeting. We can list villages which had stable populations for many generations, but have now become dormitories for larger towns or have lost half their community in the search for work. Care in the Community has foundered because the communities of many of our cities were simply not strong enough to cope.

So an urgent task of all government, both local and national, must be the strengthening of communities, through policies that enable partnership, and through legislation that supports the core communities we live in, namely our families. This will not mean extending municipal action and abolishing the constant round of charitable work, however. It will, though, mean seeking to bring an end to the debilitating isolation so many elderly people live in, releasing the imaginative ideas of so many of our voluntary organisations, and working together with local businesses to create stable local economies.

Our personal nature Our fourth principle is the personal nature of humanity, for in every sense we understand ourselves as persons in our own right. We are right to assert our individuality, for though we are framed by our culture, our family, the accidents of our birth, yet we are free. Our future is fully open yet circumscribed. Our individual talents and skills, our ingenuity and our capacity for enterprise, these cannot be frustrated. So the political system must recognise the individual, it must allow the rewarding of merit and the individual must remain accountable under the law.

Yet that is not the full extent of the significance of the personal nature of humanity. For we know that the individual will find its greatest self-expression in relation to others, within a strong community. We are designed for self-preservation, but this is not the sin that many might think. As the Earl of Shaftesbury put it, 'If a creature be self-neglectful and insensible to danger, or if he want such a degree of passion of any kind, as is useful to preserve, sustain and defend himself, this must certainly be esteemed vicious in regard of the end and design of nature.'[11] Thus even the harshest of utilitarians would have to concur that community values may be a form of enlightened self-interest. David Hume elucidated, 'The social virtues are never regarded without their beneficial tendencies nor viewed as barren and unfruitful. The happiness of mankind, the order of society, the harmony of families, the mutual support of friends, are always considered as a result of their gentle dominion over the breasts of men.'[12]

Furthermore, if our social nature is to enjoy any fruits, it will depend on the individuals within that community. As the American Pastor Reinhold Niebuhr argued in the final chapter of his book, *Moral Man and Immoral Society*, 'The most perfect justice cannot be established if the moral imagination of the individual does not seek to comprehend the needs and interests of his fellows.'[13]

Equality   The fifth principle upon which we should found our political endeavour is that of equality. Yet the very concept is more readily and frequently misunderstood than any other. For the constant fear is that in asserting that we are all equal, whether because we believe we are all created in the image of God or because it seems 'self-evident and true', we are thereby attempting to enforce some uniformity of lifestyle, of experience. Tawney argued the point,

> to criticise inequality and desire equality is not, as is sometimes suggested, to cherish the romantic illusion that

137

people are equal in character and intelligence. It is to hold that, while their natural endowments differ profoundly, it is the mark of a civilised society to aim at eliminating such inequalities as have their source, not in individual differences, but in its own organisation, and that individual differences, which are a source of social energy, are more like to ripen and find expression if social inequalities are, as far as practicable, diminished.[14]

So we are all aware of the inequalities of wealth and, more importantly, of opportunity, that result from the totally unfettered free market system. Life chances are considerably reduced for the many while the few exhaust society's resources. The rights of inheritance reinforce the effects of differences of capacity to create a fundamentally divided society. Anthony Giddens points specifically to the effects on the health of the poor,

Working-class people have on average lower birth-weight and higher rates of infant mortality, are smaller at maturity, less healthy, and die at a younger age, than those in higher class categories. Major types of mental disorder and physical illness including heart disease, cancer, diabetes, pneumonia and bronchitis are all more common at lower levels of class structure than towards the top.[15]

In other words, inequality matters. It is, as Tawney argued, not just morally indefensible, but economically impractical and inimical to the very concept of liberty that the Right would seek to defend. Any political system that seeks economic or democratic renewal must constantly reaffirm its commitment to equality.

Democracy Our sixth principle must be democracy, despite the fact that in many quarters it too is a debased theme. Thus Michael Howard, in line with the government's policy of handing more and more elements of local government over to its own appointed committees, argued for more government appointees rather than councillors on police committees because he felt that some things were too important to be left to elected representatives. But the example of South Africa, with its first free elections in 1994, must stand out as a shining example to all democratic socialists not only of the final openness of history and the possibility of change, but also of the true value of democracy and real political accountability. Yet in the British elections in May and June 1994, through apathy or disinterest turnouts were low, despite the growing trend over the years towards a higher voter turnout in local elections.

The reasons, of course, are not difficult to find, for even Conservative Council leaders who had lost their seats after many years of public service could point the finger at the government's record of broken promises and incompetence, together with an impression that political patronage and the placing of friends on quangos had undervalued our whole system.

At the same time the House of Lords is in terminal need of reform, left behind as a dinosaur in a Natural History Museum, discredited and overly prone to pomp and circumstance. Scotland and Wales have been ruled too long by the iron fist of Conservative rule in Westminster, and the regions of England have been denied the right to elect their own governments for strategic policy making. Increasingly, local government has to administer national government's policy, in education, in finance, in social services, and the locally elected councillors rarely feel a strong sense of being able to enable change. Excessive government centralisation has weakened the very sinews of democracy. Yet the concept of 'subsidiarity', so vaunted by the Conservatives in asserting Britian's rights to self-determination when it comes to Europe, rarely seems to enter their language when it comes to British local government. In 1931 Pope Pius XI wrote,

> This is a fundamental principle of social philosophy . . . Just as it is wrong to withdraw from the individual and commit to a community what private enterprise and industry can accomplish, so too it is an injustice, a grave evil and a disturbance of right order, for a large and higher association to arrogate to itself functions which can be performed efficiently by smaller and lower societies.[16]

In other words one of our principal aims must be the fostering and developing of the democratic principle, at the most local of levels, whether that be through tenants' and residents' associations, housing co-operatives, area panels, trades unions, or the Churches and other community groups.

Anger at injustice   Our final principle, and one that in many ways characterised the vision that John Smith held more clearly than any other, is that of genuine anger at injustice. Yet John Smith was not the first Labour leader to feel the same fire as inspired the prophets when he saw both natural justice abused and the natural rights of communities and individuals ignored. Kier Hardie and George Lansbury both railed against the gross injustices of the East End of London, following in the tradition of Stewart Headlam and countless other clergy who went to work in the slums of the inner cities through their commitment to the task of justice.

Today our anger must be directed at many elements of our

political system. For if Aristotle's understanding of the vital connection between equality and justice is right, then our present national life is desperately in need of reform. For Aristotle argued that political justice is manifested between those who share a common way of life 'in which they will have all that they need for an independent existence as free and equal members of society . . . Between persons who do not enjoy such freedom and equality there can be no political justice but only a simulacrum of it.'[17]

Inequality is then the source of injustice. It is felt most keenly in the unequal right of access to legal representation; the judging of one person by another because of the colour of their skin or the shape of their body; the paying of one person less than another for the same job because of their gender; the deliberate use of aggression and force to bully the weak; the refusal to grant full worker's rights to part-time workers or new employees; the holding back of wages; the banning of trades union representation at GCHQ.

All these offend a natural sense of justice, and call for measured systematic change within the context of a full renewal of our national life. As Reinhold Niebuhr said, 'Man's capacity for justice makes democracy possible, but man's inclination to injustice makes democracy necessary'[18] and it will always be within the democratic agenda that we shall seek to bring about change. Yet Nye Bevan was wrong when he said 'I know that the right kind of leader for the Labour Party is a desiccated calculating machine who must not in any way permit himself to be swayed by indignation. If he sees suffering, privation or injustice he must not allow it to move him.'[19] All of those who take a lead in politics must be moved by the world they see around them, not into precipitate and hasty judgements, but into clear, decisive and prudent action. Our defence of what is right must always be both passionate and compassionate, heart-felt and thought-through.

For in the end people's votes are guided as much by their emotions and instincts as by their rational decisions. In Gerard Manley Hopkins' phrase 'a glance master more may than gaze', precisely because we form our impressions quickly. What is required of our politics above all is that our instincts should be right, our capacity to perceive the core of a matter should be acute, and the moral basis of our project should be secure.

Finally, it is important to stress that the task of national renewal that we are engaged in is not the work of a few. For politics has been left for too long to the small cadre of professionals. Our common life, and the good of the whole community, can only be advanced if the individual aspirations and ambitions of all our fellow citizens can be harnessed. It is a corporate venture based on the most profound belief that the way things are now, the inequality, the injustice, the waste of opportunity that is now embodied in our civil life, is not inevitable. Change is possible. Our history is open-ended, and the future is yet to be written.

BIBLIOGRAPHICAL NOTES

1 P. Lilley in *Third Way*, April 1994.
2 John Smith, *Reclaiming the ground* (Spire, London, 1993), p. 128.
3 H. Wilson, speech at the Labour Party conference, 1 October 1962, quoted in *The Times* the following day.
4 W. Temple, *Christianity and the Social Order* (Penguin, London, 1942).
5 W. Temple, *Readings in St John's Gospel*, vol. 1 (Macmillan, London, 1939), introduction.
6 Commission on Social Justice, *The Justice Gap* (IPPR, London, 1993), p. 23.

7 John Donne, *Devotions*.
8 J. B. Priestley, *Time and the Conways and other plays* (Penguin, London, 1969), p. 207.
9 *Quadrogesimo anno*.
10 W. Temple, *Christianity and the social order* (Penguin, London, 1942).
11 Cited in *Social Christianity – a reader*, ed. J. Atherton (SPCK, London, 1994), p. 201.
12 *Ibid.*, p. 205.
13 R. Niebuhr, *Moral Man and Immoral Society* (SCM, London, 1963).
14 R. H. Tawney, *Equality* (George Allen & Unwin, London, 1931).
15 A. Giddens, *Sociology* (Polity Press, Cambridge, 1989), p. 215.
16 *Quadrogesimo anno*.
17 Cited in T. J. Gorringe, *Capital and the kingdom* (Orbis, New York, 1994).
18 R. Neibuhr, *Children of light and children of darkness* (Charles Scribner's Sons, New York, 1944).
19 Cited in M. Foot, *Aneurin Bevan* (MacGibbon & Co Ltd, London, 1963), vol. 2, ch. 11.